100
Activities That Build Unity, Community & Connection

Jim Cain

Other Books by Jim Cain

Teamwork & Teamplay
Raccoon Circles
Teambuilding Puzzles
A Teachable Moment
Essential Staff Training Activities
The Big Book of Low-Cost Training Games
Find Something To Do!
Rope Games
The Teamwork & Teamplay International Edition
100 Activities That Build Unity, Community & Connection

© 2017 Jim Cain and Healthy Learning. All rights reserved. Printed in the United States.

No part of this book may be reproduced, stored in a retrieval system or transmitted, in any form or by any means, electronic, mechanical, photocopying, recording, or otherwise, without the prior permission of the author, Jim Cain. Contact him at: jimcain@teamworkandteamplay.com

ISBN: 978-1-60679-374-9
Library of Congress Control Number: 2017932346
Book layout: Cheery Sugabo
Cover design: Cheery Sugabo

Healthy Learning
P.O. Box 1828
Monterey, CA 93942
www.healthylearning.com

CONTENTS

Foreword by Bob Ditter 5
Introduction by Jim Cain 9
Chapter 1: My Favorite Icebreakers 15
Chapter 2: More Icebreakers, Energizers, Get-Acquainted Games,
   and Opening Activities 43
Chapter 3: Activities That Create Teachable Moments 137
Chapter 4: Creative Debriefing and Closing Activities 175
Chapter 5: Bonus Activities 201

References, Resources & Equipment for Building Unity,
   Community & Connection 213
About Jim Cain and Teamwork & Teamplay 216

FOREWORD

Unity, Community, and Connection

Years ago when I first arrived at a boys' sailing camp on Cape Cod as a new counselor, I found myself in the middle of a group of strangers in what was affectionately known as "workweek." Workweek consisted of several days where the staff did all the things necessary to get the camp ready for the campers. We pulled boats from their winter berths, did bottom painting, put in the swimming and sailing docks, painted the boat house, swept out the cabins, carried canoes down to their summer homes by the water's edge, put up the baseball backstop, lined the fields, sprayed for poison ivy, rigged the boats, set up the mattresses, raked the pine needles off the cabins, repaired screens, and filled in all the ditches in the dirt road to camp that had formed over the winter. While I'm certain I'm leaving out scores of other tasks we did that week, I'm sure you get the picture. As I later found out, 95 percent of our time and energy would be spent on these chores.

Indeed, there were a few times throughout the week when we would gather for a short lecture about dining hall procedures, the schedule for the day, and maybe how electives worked. To me, these lectures almost seemed like a test of whether you could stay awake until the end! To the extent that we "bonded" in any way as a staff, it was through our work together. In other words, it was through happenstance. And while we did bond to some extent, and while all of our efforts on *tasks* was a great way to get us all to think about equipment and procedures, there was never any real preparation for truly working together as a team or dealing effectively with children or one another. That was typical of camps in 1974.

About 12 years later, when I made my first of over 40 visits to the wonderful camps in Mentone, Alabama, I heard my friend and long-time colleague Rob Hammond confirm this random approach to staff training. As a counselor in the late 1960s and early 1970s at the camp he eventually came to own and direct, Rob told me that during orientation the staff would trickle in from various colleges and universities from around the South and pitch in doing many of the things I had done in Massachusetts a decade earlier. He said that "orientation" was mostly about getting the camp physically ready for the campers. At the end of the week, on a Sunday morning only a few hours before the first excited and nervous campers arrived, Coach Laney would assemble the staff on the front porch of the lodge after Morning Watch and a bountiful Sunday morning brunch and give the staff his words of wisdom and instruction for the summer. What Coach said was, "Be friendly, firm, and fair!" You were now equipped with everything you needed to deal with your campers for the summer!

Some old-timers would argue that, in days gone by, the kind of "orientation" I have just described was all any honest, hard-working staff member needed in order to be effective at camp. While I won't argue the point here, I will say, things have changed! For one thing, many of the chores and projects that we used to perform as a staff are now completed by the camp maintenance crew or are undertaken well before the full staff arrive for orientation. Second, some of the behaviors we see—or at least more openly acknowledge—in campers today can be vastly complex. No longer can senior staff get away with the simple approach of Coach Laney! And finally, as camp professionals, we just know much more about people. We understand that we have a shared need to feel connected to someone we trust as a prerequisite to taking healthy risks and mastering the social, emotional, and physical lessons camp has to offer. We need to develop the "human capital" in our staff—and ourselves—in order for camp to have its maximum impact. Enter Jim Cain.

When camps first started doing icebreakers in the 1980s, it was by and large a way of breaking up the long lectures they put their counselors through during orientation. Very seldom did an icebreaker actually relate or connect in any meaningful way to what the staff would actually be doing at camp with campers and with one another. Jim Cain changed all that. To be sure, he does have an impressive array of energizers when you need one! But Jim's work goes far beyond throwing in a few activities to relieve the monotony of the talking-head approach to staff training. *Jim looks at activities as staff training!* Indeed, most of what he does is not only help people connect in more meaningful ways (see "My Favorite Icebreakers" and "More Icebreakers, Energizers, Get-Acquainted Games and Opening Activities"), he helps groups of people establish a dialogue—a consistent way of talking with one another—that will serve them well when they actually start (and finish) camp!

You can see the magic of Jim's work in his story about an activity he calls "The Big Question." In it, Jim not only describes the activity and gives us its history, he provides a rich context by sharing specific times he has used an activity with unexpected results. One such example comes from a time when Jim used "The Big Question" with a bunch of high school adolescents. When he noticed a freshman boy standing idly by without a partner, he went over and suggested that he could ask another boy—an upperclassman who just happened to be the captain of the high school football team—to be his partner. When the freshman demurred, saying the other boy was "out of his league," Jim went over to the football captain and asked him, in front of everyone there, "Are you open to anyone in this room being your next partner?" "Absolutely," the upperclassman said, and quickly waved over his younger classmate to join him. A few days later, Jim got an email from the high school principal saying that his presence and work with the students had created a major positive shift in the attitude among students toward one another. The principal told him that since he had spent time with them, the "students are mingling and sitting together everywhere. That card activity did a great job breaking down barriers between our students." It is the power of people playing together and the trust that flows from that play that Jim consistently elicits from folks; but it is also the way he prepares everyone to be successful with his approach. Unlike some presenters, who are great at what they do but whose results are incredibly difficult to replicate, Jim gives everyone the tools and the confidence to make an impact.

They say that 99.9 percent of what makes us human is something we all share. Jim Cain seems to have proven this maxim through his work with people around the world. Having given workshops and presentations in 49 states and 31 countries (so far) throughout the world, including England, Singapore, China, Japan, Colombia, Venezuela, Mexico, Spain, Portugal, Turkey, Canada, Ireland, Scotland, France, Netherlands, Wales, Bermuda, Switzerland, Indonesia, Germany, France, Italy, Denmark, Malaysia, Mongolia, Thailand, Australia, and New Zealand, Jim has shown that what moves and inspires people is universal. This book will encourage you, inspire you, and make you cry with relief that, with the right approach, maybe we all really can communicate with one another. What a gift to us all. Thank you, Jim!

—Bob Ditter

INTRODUCTION

For most of my life, being part of a group was a natural part of my world, starting with my family, my classmates, my 4-H club members, my church, my friends, and my co-workers. But very few of us actually receive any training to help us build positive relationships. Worse yet, some of the activities presented to help foster teamwork or even something as simple as breaking the ice either don't work at all or are in need of some major revamping to bring them up to the quality level our audiences deserve. Here are a few suggestions for improving your success rate with the activities presented in this book.

What's in a Name?

First of all, don't call these activities icebreakers and avoid words like teambuilding too. Unfortunately these words sometimes create negative impressions with audiences. I simply call what I do "training." When I teach a train-the-trainer workshop, I tell my audience the name of the activities I use so they know them. But when I am facilitating a program, I just launch into an activity with as little introduction as possible, and I seldom start by telling my audience the name of the activity. If it takes more than 60 seconds to explain any activity to your audience, you might try reducing the amount of information you present. If you spend five minutes teaching an activity, you will have lost a few participants along the way. Keep your introductions short, and skip telling your audience the name of any particular activity.

The Rule of Seven Minutes

I try not to allow any icebreaking activities to continue for more than seven minutes. I would much rather lead three different icebreaking activities in a single 20-minute period than to use just a single activity, even a great activity, for that length of time. The truth is, after seven minutes, you have lost the attention span of many members of your audience. Try keeping each of your icebreaker activities to seven minutes or less, and you'll see increased participation, energy, and enthusiasm from your audience. Luckily, with the volume of activities in this book, you now have a much wider selection of great activities for your next icebreaking event.

Out With the Old, In With the New

It is time to refresh your collection of icebreakers and opening activities. Make the choice to replace half of what you are currently using for icebreakers and try some new ones. I sometimes think that if I read one more description of the toilet paper icebreaker activity, I am going to scream!

So, where can you find some new ideas? Well, I just performed a search on the word "icebreakers" at Amazon and found over 1,000 books with that keyword. Read the reviews and invest in your education. And, if you want to save a few bucks on your book order, try searching the site: www.allbookstores.com. You'll find this a great site for finding the books you want at cheap prices. Oh, and if you like Amazon.com, consider using www.smile.amazon.com which is the same place, same prices, same service, but will donate a portion of your payment to the charity of your choice. Check it out.

Then, try searching the Internet using the phrase "icebreaker PDF." This will instruct your search engine to find not just icebreaking activities, but entire PDF documents filled with them. Or instead of searching the Internet based upon key words, click the "Images" button on your search engine and search for photographs and illustrations of icebreaking activities. Click on ones that you find most interesting.

Next, visit your local library or bookstore. There are plenty of good resources there. You can also enjoy the 100+ activities in this book for building unity, community, and connection. Finally, see the references and resources in the last section of this book for more ideas (and some of my favorite books filled with activities).

This Activity Doesn't Work

Have you ever heard someone say, "Yeah, I tried that activity. It doesn't work."? Instead of dropping that activity from your list of potential icebreakers, I recommend that you take the initiative to change something about the activity to improve it. For example, you can change the size of the group, or the equipment used, or the duration of the activity. Sometimes small changes in the presentation of an activity can make a big difference. Nearly every time I lead an activity, I try small variations to see if they improve the outcome. Don't be afraid to try something new, even for your favorite activities.

Social Networking Without the Internet

With so much of our social networking requiring technology these days, there is even more need for the activities in this book. Alvin Toffler wrote in his book *The Third Wave* that "high tech demands high touch" to compensate. John Naisbitt declared in his bestseller *Megatrends* that "the more high technology surrounds us, the more the need for human touch." High schools have noticed this phenomenon and have created a new form of socialization in their curricula, known as Social Emotional Learning (SEL). Many of the activities in this book are specifically presented to help you build unity, community, and connection, even in an increasingly technological world.

Which Is the Right Activity for Me?

Sometimes, facilitators ask me which activity I think they should use for a specific program. The answer is always very simple to me. You should use an activity that you are excited about. If you are excited about an activity that you are leading, your audience will be excited, and if you are not, they won't be. Simple as that.

Squeezing the Lemon

Even before you began reading this book, I am guessing that you probably already know plenty of activities. But let me explain how to get more out of these activities. I call this technique Squeezing the Lemon.

When I want to make lemonade, I take a lemon, cut it, and squeeze it. I get lemon juice. I make lemonade. Life is good! But if I squeeze that lemon harder, I can get more out of it. It's the same with the activities in this book. By working an activity harder, you and your audience can get more from them. There is certainly an element of fun in these activities, but don't be afraid to squeeze a little harder and get even more than just fun. Many of the activities in this book can help you create valuable teachable moments. Do your best to help your group find these moments, and enjoy it when you do!

The Value of Building Unity, Community & Connection

Here is a little ammunition for convincing the decision makers in your world the value of building unity, community, and connection.

Tom Rath's book *Vital Friends* provides some very helpful numbers quantifying the effect that positive relationships have within a work group. I highly recommend his book. Of the significant statistics presented, three are unforgettable. First, that teenagers spend nearly one-third of their time with friends, while the average for the rest of life is less than 10 percent. This number quantifies just how important relationships (and social networking) are to the youngest members of our culture. Secondly, 96 percent of employees with at least three close friends at work reported that they were *extremely satisfied* with their lives. Those are the people I like to work with. Finally and most importantly, the percentage of engaged employees in the general workforce is about 29 percent (with 54 percent disengaged and 17 percent actively disengaged). For employees *without* a friend at work, these numbers drop to 8 percent engaged, 63 percent disengaged, and 29 percent actively disengaged. But the good news is that for employees with a best friend at work, 56 percent are engaged! That is nearly double the average and a whopping eight times the engagement of those without friends in the workplace. Visit www.vitalfriends.org for more information about this study and the value of relationships in the workplace.

Harvey Downey, a facilitator from Great Britain shared a story related to the success rate of recruits successfully passing the basic military training of the Royal Navy. When petty officers at HMS Raleigh in Cornwall were asked what significant factors made the difference between a recruit passing or failing basic training, one drill instructor remarked, "If a recruit can make friends here or a borderline case can make even a single friend, they will probably make it through. If they do not make friends, no matter how promising they are, they will not make it!" Other instructors nodded in agreement.

The number-one factor for successfully passing basic training was to *make a friend* during the process. Those who were successful built positive relationships during their basic training period and many of those who were unsuccessful did not build friendships during this stressful period.

Ask yourself, where in my program is there an opportunity for members of my group to make a friend? If the answer is nowhere, you might want to reconsider the importance of this vital component.

The National Longitudinal Study on Adolescent Health was designed to measure factors of risk and protection for youth, with over 12,000 adolescents interviewed. The very first result presented by Michael Resnick in the *Journal of the American Medical Association* article on this study states that "parent-family connectedness and perceived school connectedness were protective against every health risk behavior measured" except one. Simply stated, if you want to protect youth in general and your youngest audience members specifically, help them feel *connected* to everyone in the room.

For more information on this study, read: "Protecting Adolescents From Harm: Findings From the National Longitudinal Study on Adolescent Health," Resnick, Bearman, Blum, Bauman, et.al., *JAMA*, September 10, 1997, Volume 278, Issue 10, pp. 823–832.

The Task, Growth, and Relationship Model

The final piece of information I'll share here presents what I call the TGR model. There are three significant components of a high-performing organization or group. Number One is a task that is worth doing. Habitat for Humanity is one example of an organization with a very worthy task. Number Two is the chance to grow and acquire new skills. No matter what role you play in an organization, the opportunity to continue to learn is a valuable component. Finally, Number Three is the opportunity to develop and maintain positive relationships in the workplace. If your organization or group has all three of these vital components, the chances that you'll have a high quality work life, better staff retention, and higher overall job satisfaction is very high. Most importantly, the lack of any one of these components is often attributed to an unsuccessful culture within an organization or group.

Think of these three ingredients as the ingredients to an organization pie. If you have all three necessary ingredients, in the right proportions, your pie tastes pretty good. But even if you have two outstanding ingredients, they will not make up for the lack of the third (necessary) ingredient. It is not enough only to give your audience a great job to do and some appropriate training to help them do it. You *absolutely* need to help them create positive relationships, too.

If you feel that the culture of your group could stand some improvement, ask yourself these questions. Which of the three components is my group missing? If I were to increase the amount of one of these components, which one would yield the greatest return and affect the greatest impact on my group's culture? Is there any component that my group is lacking, which is causing a negative shift in our culture?

And finally, if you don't happen to have any relationship-building plans for your next program, have no fear. This book alone has more than a hundred useful activities for building positive relationships with your next audience.

CHAPTER 1

My Favorite Icebreakers

Nice Icebreakers = [N]icebreakers!

This first chapter is a collection of my absolute favorite icebreakers, energizers, get-acquainted games, and opening activities. I have used them with audiences young and old, around the world. Not only are they great activities to start a program, they create wonderful teachable moments with your participants. Try one, and you'll see why they have become my favorite.

No.	Activity Name	Teachable Moment	Ideal Group Size
1	The Big Question	Open Conversation	10 or more people
2	Wrapped Around My Finger	Icebreaker	Multiple groups of 6
3	My Lifeline	Icebreaker	Multiple groups of 4 to 6
4	Where Ya From? Where Ya Been?	Geographic Icebreaker	Multiple groups of 6
5	Walking & Talking	A Moving Icebreaker	Partners
6	The Story of Your Name	Respect, Storytelling	Multiple groups of 6
7	Over Here!	Inclusion & Acceptance	Multiple groups of 6+
8	Winks, Blinks, & Belly Laughs	Eye Contact, Connection	20 or more people
9	Twice Around the Block	Icebreaker	Multiple groups of 6
10	The Story Stretch	Physical Warm-Up Activity	Multiple groups of 6 to 8

1. THE BIG QUESTION

Invite each of your participants to take (or create) a question card and find a partner. One person in each group of two reads the question on their card, and their partner answers it. Then the other partner reads the question on their card, and the first person answers it. When the conversation is complete, partners switch cards with each other (so now they each have a new question) and raise their new card high above their head (the universal sign for *I'm looking for a new partner*.) Next, form a new partnership with anyone holding a card high in the air, and the activity continues.

One of the things I like most about this activity is that, even with large groups, the actual interactions are only between two people. I also like to choose questions that are non-threatening, even for complete strangers to discuss. Here are a few examples:

What is the most unusual thing you have ever eaten? Tell me about one of your family's funniest stories. Name three things you really like about yourself. Who is the best role model you have ever met? Of all your life's accomplishments so far, of which one are you most proud? Which is your favorite pair of shoes? What is the farthest you have ever been from home? What makes your best friend your best friend? Describe a perfect day. What is something that you will never forget? Who inspires you? Who is your most unique relative, and why? What have you done that you never thought you could?

You can find 156 of these great questions on the Teamwork & Teamplay Training Cards, available from www.healthylearning.com or www.training-wheels.com, or you can collect your own questions and write them on index cards.

While facilitating The Big Question for the first day of classes at a small high school (about 180 students), I noticed one freshman boy standing quietly off to the side of the group. I looked over the crowd and suggested, "Why don't you take that guy over there as your next partner?" as I pointed to an athletic-looking senior standing nearby. "Well, that guy is the captain of our football team," he said. "I'm not really in the same league."

So I temporarily stopped the activity and walked over to the football captain and asked him, "When you raise up your card, are you open to anyone in this room being your next partner?" "Absolutely," he said, and quickly waved over his younger classman to join him.

A few days later, one of the teachers from the school emailed me and said there had been a shift in the behavior of the students in the school. "Tell me about it," I said. "Well," she said, "the cafeteria is different. In the past, students typically grouped together with the students from their same class year. Now students are mingling and sitting everywhere. That card activity did a great job breaking down barriers between our students."

The Big Question

> If you could be the star of any Hollywood movie, what movie would you choose, and what role would you play?

At the bottom of this paper write an interesting and unique question that you could ask your partner if you were to interview them for a local radio talk show. For example, you might ask questions such as:

1. What was the most unusual job you have ever had?
2. What is the definition of a life well lived?
3. Who has been the most influential person in your life, and why?

You get the idea. Keep it clean, and be creative.

When you have finished writing your question, take this paper to the center of the room, find a partner, ask them your question, (they will answer it; you do not need to write the answer down), and then they will ask you their question (you answer it). When you are both finished talking, trade papers with this person. Then find a new partner, and ask them your *new* question.

Write your question here:

You can facilitate this activity using the Teamwork & Teamplay Training Cards, pictured here. This deck of cards includes three levels of The Big Question on each card: Level One for groups that do not know each other, Level Two for groups that are somewhat familiar with each other, and Level Three for groups that know each over very well.

You can also grab a pack of index cards and create your own Big Question cards or invite your next audience to create their own cards by asking each participant to write one interesting question on an index card. If you are struggling to find good questions, there is an app for that. *Question of the Day* is (currently) a free app with a variety of interesting questions. There is also a published book version of this app, by Al Katkowksy, called Question of the Day (ISBN 978-1-59963-292-6).

Finally, you are welcome to make copies of The Big Question document on the previous page and invite your participants to create their own Big Questions. This version of The Big Question has much merit. Not only does it require your participants to engage in the process of building unity, community, and connection (by inviting them to create their own question), but it is one additional opportunity to actually use a pencil or pen and write (in their own handwriting) rather than texting or typing. In our high tech world, penmanship may be an antiquated art, but it remains a valuable and fundamental form of personal expression.

When the Association for Experiential Education (AEE) national conference came to Rochester, New York, a few years ago, I was asked to present an opening workshop for about 300 people. When the time came for my workshop to begin, only about 80 people were present, as others continued to slowly trickle in from other locations. Rather than start an activity and then restart (and re-explain) it every time more people joined us, I had a better plan.

I invited the 80 or so folks in the room to each take an index card and write down a question they could ask someone if they were interviewing them for a local radio talk show. Then I instructed them how to play The Big Question. Next, I stood in the doorway, and as more participants joined us, I simply handed them an index card and said (as I pointed to the group in the middle of the room already engaged in the activity), "Ask them what to do."

Participants entered the room and were immediately pulled into the game, and those already playing were glad to help newcomers with their question cards and the rules of the game.

2. WRAPPED AROUND MY FINGER

Invite participants (in groups of six people) to take turns introducing themselves to their group, while wrapping a long piece of string (such as ordinary cotton packaging twine) or Raccoon Circle (see photo) around their index finger as they talk. A 15-foot (4.6 meter) piece of string or webbing will require about a minute's worth of conversation to wrap around their finger. Each speaker is invited to continue talking until they have completely wrapped the string (or webbing) around their finger. When finished, the speaker unrolls the string or webbing and transfers it to the next person in the group.

A Raccoon Circle is a 15-foot (4.6 meter) long segment of 1-inch (25.4mm) wide tubular climbing webbing, available in many camping stores and occasionally in marine/hardware stores or horse tack shops. This webbing comes in a variety of colors and patterns and is extremely durable. It is also one of the few teambuilding props that I have discovered that works fine when wet. So even a rainy day won't stop this icebreaker.

For more Raccoon Circle activities, see *The Revised and Expanded Book of Raccoon Circles* (ISBN 978-0-7575-3265-8) by Jim Cain and Tom Smith, available from www.healthylearning.com and www.kendallhunt.com, and download a free PDF document filled with Raccoon Circle activities from www.teamworkandteamplay.com/resources.html.

During a conference in Malaga, Spain, one participant modified this activity and instead of a using a piece of string or Raccoon Circle, she told us a story while peeling an apple. Which brings up a good point in this book. You are welcome to make safe modifications to any of the activities in this book if it helps you build unity, community, and connection with your participants.

I am told that there is an educational theory that explains why the kinesthetic act of wrapping a piece of string (or webbing) around your finger (or any manual manipulation) occupies the part of your brain that controls nervousness. I have noticed that this particular activity makes it very easy for people to share with the members of their group. I have also noticed that you can actually learn quite a bit about the person by watching their wrapping technique. Some people talk and forget to wrap. Some people wrap and forget to talk. Some participants wrap very, very carefully, so their webbing is neat and orderly. Some wrap haphazardly and often end up with a tangled mess. Sometimes, if the previous person passes the webbing in a tangle, participants may have a more difficult time wrapping it around their finger. Often, I see other members of the group come to their rescue, untangling the webbing as the story continues.

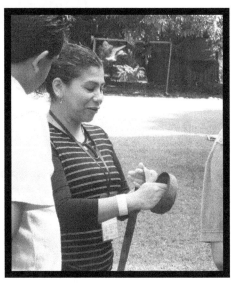

The first time I saw a version of this activity was at a recreation workshop.* Participants were each invited to take a piece of yarn and then assemble in small groups of about eight people. Each person was then instructed to introduce themselves to the group while winding their piece of yarn around their finger. The intent was that each person would continue to talk until they completed wrapping the length of yarn they had chosen around their index finger.

Some participants had taken a very small length of yarn and so their introductions were quite brief. Others, who had taken several feet of yarn, were challenged to find interesting facts to tell as they continued winding.

I decided to make two significant modifications to this activity. First, I discovered that when you tightly wrap a significant amount of yarn around your index finger, it tends to cut off the circulation and your finger turns blue. So I switched from yarn to one of my favorite teambuilding props, a Raccoon Circle (made from colorful tubular climbing webbing). Next, because participants tend to select different lengths of yarn, the time necessary for each person varies widely. For this concern, I chose a standard length of 15 feet (4.6 meters) for my Raccoon Circles so that each person has about a minute to introduce themselves while winding the webbing around their finger.

*There are many recreation leadership workshops in the United States. These workshops are excellent ways to acquire skills as a recreation leader in a variety of subjects, such as dancing, quilting, teambuilding, crafts, singing, storytelling, outdoor cooking, puppetry, and many, many more. Some of my favorite workshops include:

Buckeye (Ohio) Leadership Workshop, www.buckeyeleadership.org

Hoosier (Indiana) Recreation Workshop, www.hoosierrecreation.com

Great Lakes (Michigan) Recreation Leaders lab, www.greatlakesreclab.com

Black Hills (South Dakota) Recreation Leaders Laboratory, www.bhrll.org

3. MY LIFELINE

In this activity, groups of four to six people gather around a visual model of their lifeline (the entire chronology of their life). This line can be made of rope or string (or Raccoon Circle webbing) or masking tape, or perhaps a permanent line such as those found on a basketball court, sidewalk, parking lot, or tile floor.

The opportunity in this activity is for each member of the group to share some of the most significant events (milestones) in their life as they walk along the length of their lifeline. There obviously isn't time to tell everything that has happened to them, only the most significant and important events. As the speaker walks along the lifeline model, the other members of the group walk with them, joining them on their journey.

When the speaker reaches the present day location, they are encouraged to share something they are looking forward to in the future. Then, the next member of the group can begin to share the elements of their lifeline.

I have noticed that some icebreakers are static. That is, participants tend to stand in the same place during these activities. One of the aspects of My Lifeline that I particularly like is the movement for not only the speaker in this activity, but every member of the group. It feels like more of a journey (with friends) when your group follows you as you walk through some of your favorite memories and key milestones in your life.

Another feature of this activity, especially when working with young people, is what happens when each speaker reaches the present day location and tells their group about their plans for the future. Future vision, looking ahead, having a plan, optimism, and hopefulness are all part of what psychologist Carol Dweck refers to as mindset, which has a definitive effect on the quality of your life. For more information, see the book *Mindset: The New Psychology of Success* (ISBN 978-0-3454-7232-8).

Finally, one group member mentioned to me that his lifeline was not a straight line. There was a time in his life when he "got a little off track" and so he demonstrated this by bending the Raccoon Circle lifeline. Our group followed him down his non-linear path and learned about some significant events that turned his life around. I realized then how powerful this activity could be.

You can find this activity and many more in the book *Rope Games* (ISBN 978-0-9882046-1-4) by Jim Cain, available from www.healthylearning.com and www.training-wheels.com.

4. WHERE YA FROM? WHERE YA BEEN?

This Raccoon Circle activity starts with groups of six people holding a knotted Raccoon Circle in their hands. One at a time, each person invites the other members of the group to help them create a visual map of the city, county, state, or nation where they are from, or they can create a map of a location that they have recently visited. This same person then discusses what it was like to grow up in this location, or what it was like to travel to this place. Next, other members of the group are invited to ask questions about this location or add their own insights if they have visited the same place.

I like to ask that groups create the map in the air, with all group members holding the perimeter of the Raccoon Circle. This connection keeps the group members engaged and interested in the story. Occasionally, I observe a group that places the Raccoon Circle on the floor, and I have noticed that the members of such a group become disconnected spectators rather than engaged and connected group members.

I have also observed that speakers from mountainous regions of the world sometimes create three-dimensional maps (showing elevation, geography, and topology). This is a very creative interpretation of the activity, indeed.

This activity is an example of one that I did not create, but rather observed as it created itself. I was presenting a workshop for the Association of Experiential Education (AEE) at their Mid-Atlantic regional conference. I was leading a series of Raccoon Circle activities in small groups of eight people. In between activities, I overheard one group discussing where everyone was from. One person in this particular group was from Scotland. When another person in the group mentioned that he didn't exactly know where that was, the Scottish group member took the knotted Raccoon Circle and invited the other members of the group to help him make a map of England and Scotland and then began pointing to the map at the various places he had lived and traveled. Several other members of the group had also visited Scotland and added their stories and locations to the discussion, and as a result, a brand new activity was born.

You can find this activity and many more in the book *Rope Games* (ISBN 978-0-9882046-1-4) by Jim Cain, available from www.healthylearning.com and www.training-wheels.com.

5. WALKING & TALKING

This icebreaker requires no equipment at all. Begin by inviting everybody to find a partner and link elbows. Next, instruct each pair to take a stroll together and find three things that they have in common—the more unique or unusual the commonality, the better. This combination of walking and talking is an active way to move a group and to encourage the group to focus on what they have in common. You can also use this activity when you are moving a group from Point A to Point B. Explain the activity, and then invite them to find commonalities as they walk from here to there.

For some groups, especially those with significant diversity, it can be easy to point out the differences between the members of the group. This activity focuses on those things that we have in common, even with people from significantly different backgrounds, locations, cultures, and communities.

Over the years, I have witnessed dozens of participants finding unique and interesting commonalities with their partners. Some of my favorites include two social services workers in Missouri that discovered they had both grown up in the same state, the same county, the same city, and on the same street (but at different times in their lives). It turns out they had lived on the same street, four houses apart, but during different decades. What a fun connection.

Next were the two women from California that met at one of my workshops and discovered during this activity that each of them had three children, and their three children had the same first three names! It was not surprising to find these two women eating meals together and hanging out during the workshop. They had found something unique that they both had in common.

Another interesting connection story came from two college students in Chicago. After finding two connections, one woman turned to her partner and said, "I think I've been in your apartment! Last semester, your roommate and I had a class together, and we worked on a project one weekend in your apartment. I don't think you were around then, but I've been to your house!"

You can find this activity and many more in *The Teamwork & Teamplay International Edition* (ISBN 978-0-9882046-3-8) by Jim Cain, available from www.healthylearning.com and www.training-wheels.com.

6. THE STORY OF YOUR NAME

An activity that builds respect around people's names is a great way to foster unity, community, and connection. I typically like to conduct this activity in a single group, provided time is available. If not, you are welcome to facilitate this activity in several smaller groups.

Many of us know the story of how we came to have our name. Some of us were named after relatives, famous people, or friends of our family. The Story of Your Name is your chance to share how you came to have your name. What you like about it, and any stories you want to tell about your name. At the very end of your story, you are invited to tell the group what name you would like to be called, and the group will practice calling you by this name.

If someone were to say, "Well, you can call me Dave or David, it doesn't really matter," I would say to that person, "What would you prefer? It is your choice." But choose wisely. I once had a camp staff member who said, "My name is Bob, but you can call me Captain Jack," and for the rest of the summer, he was Captain Jack!

The Story of Your Name is an opportunity to build respect by pronouncing the names of each member in your group correctly. As our world becomes increasingly more diverse, we have to work harder to learn and correctly pronounce the names of those we meet.

Of the many activities in this book, the Story of Your Name is one of the most powerful. Here are some of my favorite stories connected with this activity.

A summer camp counselor shared this story:

> Just after my parents were married, they were traveling internationally. My dad is the kind of guy that, if someone is asking for money, he always gives something. On market day, my parents were shopping in different places. My dad encountered a guy who was begging for money, and true to his word, he reached into his wallet to pull out some money. But since he was traveling, he only had some fairly large currency. But he always gave something, so he gave the beggar one of these large denomination bills. The beggar invited him to sit down, and asked him about his life. "Tell me about your son," he said. "I don't have a son yet," my dad said, "my wife and I are just recently married." "You will," said the man, and told him his future son's name. "Tell me about your daughter." "I don't have a daughter yet." "You will," said the man, and told my dad my future sister's name.

> Then my dad said that he would really like my mother to hear this conversation, and told the man that he would find her and quickly come back. When he returned, the man was gone, the chairs were gone, no one there could remember seeing the man; he just vanished. And my parents had a son and a daughter, and gave us the names the beggar had told my dad.

While training teachers from a private school in Massachusetts, including an international exchange teacher from China, this story was shared:

> Each year, our school tries to hire a visiting teacher from a different part of the world. This year, a teacher from China joined us. "The closest name in English to my official name in China is Ralph," said the professor, "so you can call me Ralph." But the other members of the faculty, understanding how important it was (culturally), simply said, "No, we'd like to call you by your real name. We just need you to help us practice saying it correctly." And so he did. The teachers had done a great thing, and I'm sure their students did as well.

A group leader pulled this activity from my book *Find Something To Do!* and shared this story:

> We recently created a safe place for discussing the needs of the transgender population in our community. Over the course of a weekend, we invited members of the community, allies, families, friends, teachers, and community leaders to join in a series of workshops and informational sessions. As an icebreaker on Friday night, I facilitated the Story of Your Name as one of the opening activities. Unfortunately, we had many more participants than expected, and we ran out of time Friday night before everyone had the opportunity to speak. But the next morning at breakfast, some participants rose and spontaneously began to tell the story of their names. In the transgender community, the name you choose is very closely tied to your identity and is very significant. Over the course of the rest of the weekend, mostly at meals, participants continued to share the story (and identity) of their names. It became the most powerful activity of the entire weekend.

You can find this activity and many more in the book *Find Something To Do* (ISBN 978-0-9882046-0-7) by Jim Cain, available from www.healthylearning.com and www.training-wheels.com.

7. OVER HERE!

Over Here is one of my favorite activities for large groups, and it creates an atmosphere of energy and inclusion that can last well beyond the activity.

Begin by forming groups of 10 people. You can place each group inside the perimeter of a knotted Raccoon Circle that has been placed on the ground, or simply invite each group to stand closely together and slightly apart from other groups. Next, identify a specific characteristic (such as the tallest person) for each group. Inform the group that on the count of 1-2-3, they are to wave goodbye to the tallest person in each group and say, "See ya!"

At this point, the tallest person in each group becomes a free agent, leaving their original group, and seeking a new group to join. But each group has lost one of their teammates. In order to get a replacement, instruct each group to yell, "Over here, over here!"

There are a few ground rules for this activity. First, it is okay for participants to return to their original group. Second, groups can invite more than one person to join them. Third, it is okay to go out and recruit new members. But there is a difference between recruitment and kidnapping! Recruitment is non-contact, so you can invite people to join your group, you just cannot grab them and pull them into your circle.

Some useful categories for this activity include: tallest person in each group, the person wearing the most jewelry, the person with the cleanest shoes, the two people with the longest and shortest hair, the person with the most brothers and sisters, the person with the biggest hands, etc.

I noticed that after playing this game for a summer camp staff training event, whenever the camp staff needed more people for an activity, they often yelled out, "Over here, over here!" It seems the inclusiveness of this game extended well beyond the game itself. And after a few days, even campers began chanting "Over here!" whenever they wished to invite more people to join their group. In the introduction for this book, I mentioned the concept of "squeezing the lemon," or getting more out of an activity than just the game itself. Over Here has the potential to create an atmosphere of inclusion in a group that lasts long after the game is finished!

This activity comes from the creative mind of Chris Cavert (www.fundoing.com) I am extremely grateful to have Chris as a colleague, co-author, and friend. Chris has a bunch of great books, including *Affordable Portables* and *50 Ways to Use Your Noodle*, both available from www.healthylearning.com and www.wnbpub.com.

8. WINKS, BLINKS, AND BELLY LAUGHS

Invite each member of your group to secretly choose a number from one to five. Next, ask them to mingle around the crowd and to wink that number of times when they meet another person. If the other person winks the same number of times, link elbows. If they wink a different number of times, no problem, they are just part of another group. Continue until everyone has found a partner in this first round of the game. At this point, I like to ask the various linked groups to reply, "Yee-haw" when I call their number.

In Round Two, ask participants to choose a new number from one to five, but instead of winking (one eye), participants find their partners by blinking (both eyes). Continue until everyone has found their people. This time, ask groups to respond, "Woo-haw" when their number is called.

In the final round, Round Three, ask participants to choose a different number from one to five, and this time to find their partners by placing both hands on their stomach, and loudly laughing that number of times. When everyone has found their "belly laugh" partners, invite them to laugh that number of times when their number is called.

One of my favorite moments in this game happened near the end of Round One (the winking round) when one string of people met an individual without a team. Even though the individual winked a different number of times than that rest of the team, one participant reached out, linking elbows with the individual and said, "Close enough!" Not even the rules of the game could keep these folks from forming connection. Well done.

Twenty years ago, Michael Resnick presented the findings of the National Longitudinal Study on Adolescent Health concerning the engagement in risky behaviors of the youth in our communities. Such risks include: alcoholism, drug use, suicide, violence, and more. Two very significant results emerged from this study. Parent/Family connectedness and perceived school connectedness protected students (grades 7-12) from seven out of eight of the community risk factors. When students are connected, they do not engage in risky behaviors that often come with negative outcomes. So in this activity, when you connect with another person, and link to them, you say, "You are one of ours!" That behavior has been shown in this study to have a positive effect on the lives of those participating in the connection. We are not just playing a game here; we are protecting our youngest participants from risky behaviors! For more information about this study, see the article "Protecting Adolescents From Harm" in the *Journal of the American Medical Association (JAMA)*, September 10, 1997, Volume 278, Issue 10, page 823.

I learned this activity from Chris Cavert (www.fundoing.com) and Sam Sikes (www.doingworks.com)—two amazing authors, facilitators, teachers and trainers in the adventure-based learning world.

9. TWICE AROUND THE BLOCK

Have you ever participated in an icebreaking activity when one member of the group just went on and on and on? Twice Around the Block is the perfect antidote for this situation. In this activity, the group decides how much time the speaker is allowed to talk.

Begin by inviting each circle of six people to grasp a knotted Raccoon Circle in their hands. The person nearest the knot is the first speaker. The activity begins with this person letting go of the Raccoon Circle. As the speaker introduces themselves to the group, the rest of the group uses their hands to slowly pass the knot around the circle to the right. When it comes back to the speaker the first time, that's once around the block. When it comes back to the speaker the second time, the speaker's time is up.

If the group is enjoying the speaker, they may choose to move the knot slowly around the circle. But if they just wish the speaker would finish, they can move more quickly. At this point, the speaker passes the knot to another member of the group, and the activity continues.

A Raccoon Circle is a 15-foot (4.6 meter) segment of 1-inch (2.54 cm) wide tubular climbing webbing, available in many camping stores and occasionally in marine/hardware stores or horse tack shops. This webbing comes in a variety of colors and patterns and is extremely durable. It is also one of the few teambuilding props that I have discovered that works fine when wet. So even a rainy day won't stop this icebreaker.

For more Raccoon Circle activities, see *The Revised and Expanded Book of Raccoon Circles* (ISBN 978-0-7575-3265-8) by Jim Cain and Tom Smith, available from www.healthylearning.com and www.kendallhunt.com, and download a free PDF document filled with Raccoon Circle activities from www.teamworkandteamplay.com/resources.html.

10. THE STORY STRETCH

One person in each circle of eight people begins this activity by telling a story that includes motions. The other members of the group follow their leader and replicate their movements exactly. After 30 to 60 seconds, the next person in the group continues the story in a new direction (again with movements repeated by the other members of the group). Continue until each member of the group has had the opportunity to share their story and movements.

The Story Stretch is not only an excellent warm-up activity and energizer, it also incorporates leadership and storytelling. Just watch the next time you facilitate this activity, and you'll easily spot the great storytellers and leaders in each group.

If you happen to incorporate yoga stretches in your mindfulness program, you can use the Story Stretch as a way of sharing the leadership in these stretches.

I first learned this activity from the staff of the Albuquerque, New Mexico YMCA Leadership Camp. When I arrived at camp, the director handed me two sleeping bags. I was thinking that one sleeping bag was probably sufficient when the director informed me that temperatures in the mountains south of Albuquerque often plummeted at night. In the morning, campers were a bit chilly, but rather than complain about it, the staff found an outstanding way to warm them up and get them ready for the day. And, even better, their technique also incorporated leadership.

Each morning, groups would gather outside the dining hall and begin The Story Stretch. One person in each group would begin to tell a story and each story had movements. As the leader told the story, each member of the group would mimic their actions. Then, after about 30 seconds, the next person in the group would continue the story, often taking it in some new direction, with even more movements. By the time the last person in each group finished their movements and story, the group was warmed-up, everyone had had the opportunity to be a leader, and the group was energized and ready for the day.

You can find this activity and many more in *The Big Book of Low-Cost Training Games* (ISBN 978-0-07-177437-6) by Mary Scannell and Jim Cain, available from www.healthylearning.com and www.mhprofessional.com.

CHAPTER 2

More Icebreakers, Energizers, Get-Acquainted Games and Opening Activities

This chapter contains even more icebreakers, energizers, physical warm-ups, get acquainted games, and opening activities, many that can be facilitated with minimal props and several using the easy-to-copy pages included in their activity description

No.	Activity Name	Teachable Moment	Ideal Group Size
11	Are You More Like?	Icebreaker, Making Choices	10 or More People
12	Believe It or Knot	Icebreaker, Self-Disclosure	Multiple Groups of 6
13	Have You Ever?	Active Icebreaker, Discovery	Groups of 10 to 50
14	Do You Like Your Neighbor?	Active Icebreaker, Discovery	Groups of 10 to 50
15	Goal Lines	Goal Setting Activity	Any
16	X Marks the Spot	Pre-Game Warm-Up Activity	10 or More People
17	The Gathering Place	Welcome Activity	Any
18	Doodles	Creativity	5 or More People
19	Group Photographs	Capturing History	Any
20	Fortune Cookies	Random Questions	Any
21	That Person Over There	Icebreaker, Memory	10 or More People
22	Concentric Circles	Conversation	10 or More People
23	Smartphone Activities	Digital Icebreakers	Partners/Small Groups
24	What Is in Your Pocket?	Personal History	Partners/Small Groups
25	Four Corners	Discovery, Icebreaker	15 or More People
26	Statistical Treasure Hunt	Discovery, Match	Multiple Small Groups
27	First Impressions	Icebreaker	Trios of 3 People

No.	Activity Name	Teachable Moment	Ideal Group Size
28	Autographs	Icebreaker	10 or More People
29	Hieroglyphics	An Intelligent Icebreaker	Multiple Small Groups
30	Commonalities	Connection	24 or more people
31	Face to Face / Back to Back	Conversation	Partners
32	The Walk of Life	Active Icebreaker	Trios of 3 People
33	Handshakes	Icebreaker	10 or More People
34	All My Life's a Circle	Circular Storytelling	Multiple Groups of 6
35	Core Groups	Unity, Connection	Multiple Groups of 6+
36	Mingle	Commonalities	20 or More People
37	Change Three Things	Observations, Memory	Partners
38	The Big Answer	Finding the Answers	10 or More People
39	Kerfuffle	A Chaotic Icebreaker	20 or More People
40	Mixer Dances	A Musical Mixer	20 or More People
41	The Morning Dance Party	Energizer, Warm-Up	10 or More People
42	The Imaginary Obstacle Course	Warm-Up Activity	Multiple Groups of 6+
43	Boogie Ball	Musical Warm-Up	Multiple Groups of 6+
44	The Meter	Group Discovery	Any
45	Stationary Greetings	Connection	10 or More People
46	Truly Unique	Uniqueness	Any
47	Mint Condition	Icebreaker	Any

No.	Activity Name	Teachable Moment	Ideal Group Size
48	Favorite Scar Stories	Personal History	Any
49	Magic Lamp	Make a Wish	Any
50	Five Photos	Imaginary Slideshow	Any
51	My Personal Pyramid	Discovery, Insight	4 or More People
52	Metaphorically Speaking	Creativity	10 or More People
53	Best / Worst / First	Icebreaker	Multiple Groups of 6
54	Acronyms & Abbreviations	An Intelligent Icebreaker	Multiple Small Groups
55	Draw Me Your Story	Artistic Storytelling	Partners/Small Groups
56	End-of-the-Day Questions	Goal Setting	Any
57	Five Events That Shaped My Life	Icebreaker	Partners/Small Groups
58	Broken Token	Finding Your People	Partners
59	Emotional Weather Report	Creative Opener	Any
60	Backside Writing	Hysterical Introductions	Any
61	Captain Nemo	Energizer	20 to 30 People
62	The Box	Artistic Self Discovery	Partners/Small Groups
63	Balloon Bop for Three	Warm-Up Activity	Trios of 3 People
64	Choo-Choo, Who Are You?	Active Group Formation	30 or More People
65	Story Tags	Creative Storytelling	Any
66	Hall of Fame Statues	Creative Opening Activity	Multiple Groups of 6

11. ARE YOU MORE LIKE?

This activity is a variation of The Big Question, found earlier in this book. For this variation, participants are asked to make a choice. Explanations are not required, but invited. For example, "Which are you more like: a sparkler or a firecracker?"

Invite each of your participants to take (or create) a question card and find a partner. One person in each group of two reads the question on their card, and their partner answers it. Then the other partner reads the question on their card, and the first person answers it. When the conversation is complete, partners switch cards with each other (so now they each have a new question) and raise their new card high above their head (the universal sign for I'm looking for a new partner.) Next, form a new partnership with anyone holding a card high in the air and the activity continues.

Here are a few examples of questions for this activity. Are you more like:

- Bookstores or Libraries
- Words or Numbers
- PC or Mac
- Car or Truck
- Odd or Even
- Text Message or Voice Message
- Software or Hardware
- A Firecracker or a Sparkler
- Dine In or Carry Out
- Professional Sports or Amateur Sports
- Walking or Running
- Window or Aisle
- Weekday or Weekend
- Star Wars or Star Trek
- Day or Night

You can find dozens of these questions on the Teamwork & Teamplay Training Cards, available from www.healthylearning.com or www.training-wheels.com, and even more in the book, *Are You More Like? 1001 Colorful Quandaries for Quality Conversations* (ISBN 978-1-8854-7341-9) by Chris Cavert and Susana Acousta available from www.wnbpub.com.

12. BELIEVE IT OR KNOT

Occasionally, people will surprise you with the information they share about themselves. Believe it or Knot is a Raccoon Circle activity that invites participants to reveal information about themselves in a fun and creative manner.

Begin this activity with groups of six people grasping a knotted Raccoon Circle. Using their hands, invite the group to pass the knot to the right around the circle. "To the right, to the right, to the right, now, stop!" The person nearest the knot becomes the first speaker.

The speaker tells the group something interesting about themselves. This information can be true, or it could be false. After sharing this information, the other members of the group can ask the speaker a total of three questions, then they have to decide whether to believe them or not. After the group votes, the speaker reveals the truth and then passes the knot to another person, and the activity continues.

Some of the more interesting things I have heard during this activity (all of which turned out to be true) include: I was named after my grandfather's dog. I really have a super power. I have a hyper immune system, which means I have never been sick a day I my life. And the most unusual so far: my heart is on the opposite side of where it should be! What interesting thing can you add to the list of unique Believe It or Knot revelations?

There is a variation of Believe It or Knot that has been around for a long, long time, known as Two Truths and a Lie. In this no-prop version of the activity, participants are invited to share three interesting things about themselves, two of which are true and a third that is false. Other members of the group must then discuss and decide which of the three items they believe is false. After their decision, the current speaker reveals which two of their three items are true and which one is false.

A Raccoon Circle is a 15-foot (4.6 m) long segment of 1-inch (25.4mm) wide tubular climbing webbing, available in many camping stores and occasionally in marine/hardware stores or horse tack shops. This webbing comes in a variety of colors and patterns and is extremely durable.

For more Raccoon Circle activities, see *The Revised and Expanded Book of Raccoon Circles* (ISBN 978-0-7575-3265-8) by Jim Cain and Tom Smith, and the book *Rope Games* (ISBN 978-0-9882046-1-4) by Jim Cain. Both are available from www.healthylearning.com and www.training-wheels.com.

13. HAVE YOU EVER?

In this active icebreaker, participants form a large circle with each person standing on some type of place-marker, such as an index card, plastic spot marker, or other flat object. One person stands inside the circle, on an easy-to-see different colored place-marker, and becomes the first speaker. Next they say the phrase, "Have You Ever…?" and complete the sentence by sharing something that is true for them. "Have You Ever… played sports in high school?"

At this point, anyone in the group that has played a sport in high school must change location. While each person is seeking a new location to stand, the speaker also attempts to find a new location. At the completion of each round, one person will be without a place to stand in the circle and becomes the new speaker for the next round.

Two variations I like for this activity include inviting the speaker to introduce themselves and the entire group saying hello to them in return, and anytime a speaker has done something that no one else in the group has done, they receive a standing ovation of applause from the group.

I also like to give the speaker a very visible location to stand, just inside the perimeter of the circle. A speaker in the center has their back to 50 percent of the circle at any time. Near the perimeter, the speaker has a better chance of being heard.

As a facilitator, I like to include myself in this game whenever I play it, for a very valuable reason. I sometimes play with audiences where occasionally the subject matter revealed in Have You Ever can shift to things that some may consider inappropriate for this format of activity. If this happens, I simply become the speaker for the next round, and from this central position, encourage the group to focus their efforts on more appropriate levels of disclosure.

14. DO YOU LIKE YOUR NEIGHBOR?

Here is another game from my childhood. Form a large circle with players standing on some type of place-marker, such as an index card, or seated in chairs. One player (without a place marker) is designated the leader and circulates about the center of the circle. The leader randomly approaches a player in the circle and while facing them says, "Do you like your neighbor?" This player, looking left and right at their neighbors can answer in two distinct ways. If they answer, "Yes, I like my neighbors very much," the leader smiles and moves on. But if they answer "No," the leader asks, "Who would you prefer to have as your neighbor?" The player then can choose one of many possibilities, such as, "I would prefer neighbors with blue jeans," at which point everyone in the circle wearing blue jeans must chance locations. Or they might say, "I prefer neighbors that speak a foreign language" or "I prefer neighbors that have read all the Artemis Fowl books" or even "I prefer everyone to be my neighbor."

As players move about, the leader may try to take one of the available spaces, requiring a new player to become the leader in the next round of the game.

Another variation of this game is called The Big Wind Blows. A leader stands in the center of the circle and says, "The big wind blows for everyone wearing socks," at which point everyone in the circle wearing socks must change places. After two or three rounds, the leader tries to take one of the available spaces in the circle, and a new leader continues the game.

One final variation of this activity is called Upset the Fruit Basket. In this version, players are seated in a circle of chairs. Players are designated one of four fruits: apples, peaches, grapes, and bananas. If the leader calls out, "Apples," then all apples must change places. If the leader calls out, "Grapes and bananas," both of these fruits must change places. But if the leader calls out, "upset the fruit basket," everyone must change places.

Early in my career, I facilitated a pre-conference workshop for the Virginia Council of Outdoor Education and the Mid-Atlantic Association for Experiential Education near Richmond, Virginia. After a full day of adventure-based learning, the 20 or so participants in my workshop and I discovered that there was no program that evening (the official start of the conference was the following morning). So after dinner, we gathered together and began playing all the no-prop games we could remember. I remember leading Upset the Fruit Basket and was surprised to learn that no one in the group had ever played that game before.

15. GOAL LINES

Take a short piece of rope, and tie three overhand knots (one at each end and one in the middle). Next, place this rope in a straight line on the ground (floor) in front of you, and tell your group that the three knots represent the beginning, middle, and end of your program. Then invite the members of your group to discuss where they are at the beginning of the program, where they hope to be at the mid-point and a goal they have for the end of the program.

For example, a participant might mention that at the beginning of the program they do not know the names of everyone in the group. By the mid-point, they hope to know more people by name, and by the end of the day, they hope to know everyone in the group by name.

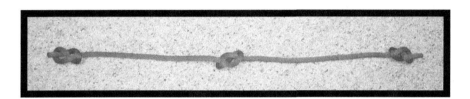

While you can conduct this activity for your group with a single piece of rope, you might consider providing a single piece of rope for every member of the group, and placing these ropes in a circle (like spokes of a wheel). At the beginning of the experience, participants can discuss their individual goals. The Goal Lines can be revisited halfway through the event as a mid-point checkup. As a final reviewing activity, participants can simultaneously walk along their Goal Line, from the outer knot (beginning of the day) to the inner knot (the completion of the day) and gather together in the center as one group to celebrate their achievements.

In the world of adventure-based learning, teaching, and training, Roger Greenaway is a shining example of talent, resourcefulness, and extreme generosity. Roger literally gives away his best ideas for processing, debriefing, reviewing, and reflection at his website: www.reviewing.co.uk. You can find more of Roger's contributions to the world of reviewing in my book *A Teachable Moment*, and in Roger's book *Active Reviewing* (available from Amazon.com). A few years ago, I shared some Raccoon Circle activities with a UK adventure-based learning publication (*Horizons* magazine), which inspired Roger to create some reviewing techniques with short pieces of rope for the next issue of that publication. Goal Lines was just one of the valuable ideas Roger generated for his article.

You can find this activity and more opening activities in the book *Rope Games* (ISBN 978-0-9882046-1-4) by Jim Cain, available from www.healthylearning.com and www.training-wheels.com.

Recently I found myself in Portland, Oregon, near the location of my favorite bookstore in the whole world: Powell's City of Books (www.powells.com). The store takes up an entire block of downtown Portland. If you have been there, then you know it is an amazing place, and if you have not been there, you should definitely go! Anyway, just outside Powell's bookstore, if you look carefully, you can find some pretty amazing things, including a whole block of food cart vendors featuring food from around the world. But I happened to find something else. Framed in neat silver letters at the top of one building, I found the slightly disconcerting phrase "PANIC." For those of us who have read Douglas Adam's *The Hitchhiker's Guide to the Galaxy*, we know that the cover of *Hitchhiker's Guide* has nice, friendly letters spelling out the words "Don't Panic." Well, it turns out that PANIC is actually a shockingly good software company. But look around. You may find some interesting things indeed.

Which brings me to the last commentary about being aware of your surroundings, as prompted by the activity X Marks the Spot. In many places Geocaching (geocaching.com) has become a worldwide phenomenon. You can even search city by city to find clues about the location of caches in urban areas, public spaces, wilderness areas, and more. Happy hunting!

16. X MARKS THE SPOT

Here is an activity that early arrivals can play before your program begins. Place a small object such as a coin, wooden letter, or small toy somewhere in your activity space. Then invite everyone in your group to casually search the area, looking for—but not moving—the object. When they have discovered the location of the object, they can take a seat.

Depending on the observations skills of your group, you can modify the size of the object used in this activity. I like to use wooden letters available at most craft stores. Coins of various sizes work well too. There are even artists that place found art in their workshops and wait to see who will discover them during the event. You can search Pinterest for many more examples of found art.

When I was a kid and found myself at the dentist's office, they occasionally had *Highlights* magazine. One of the features of the magazine was a line drawing of a scene in which various familiar objects (a hammer, a face, a chair) would be carefully drawn into the scenery. A list of all the "hidden" objects was provided, and I tried to find as many objects as I could. For your next event, take a photograph of a dozen or so objects (make copies of this photo for each search party group), and then place these objects around your meeting location. Before the program begins, invite everyone that arrived early to form small groups and search for these objects (but do not move them from their hiding place). You have now created a 3-D treasure hunt. In addition to the photograph of objects, you can also provide a clue for each object. Such as, "The thing you seek is near a week" for an object you hide near a calendar. Happy hunting!

For many years, Reverend Gabe Campbell was the featured speaker at the Ohio State 4-H Leadership Camp. Gabe had an amazing collection of group activities and was one of the first speakers I witnessed who combined group dynamics, games, storytelling, and training in one amazing experience. One morning at this camp, we all gathered together for a session with Gabe. Chairs had been placed in pods of three throughout the training space, but before we found a seat, Gabe asked us to walk around until we found a nickel he had placed somewhere on the floor (without giving away the location to anyone else). For several minutes the group milled about, until one by one, people began to take their seats. Eventually everyone found the nickel and a seat, and the program officially started. Gabe pointed out that if we are observant, and know what we are looking for, we just might find it—and he used that metaphor as the start of his workshop. *A teachable moment*, indeed.

At the beginning of your next event, ask your participants to search the area and count the number of times they find something red. Then, when the group is finished and assembled, ask them how many things they found that were green. Often the answer is "Zero" or "I don't know." When we are focused on finding one thing, we often disregard or neglect the other great things that might come our way. To prove this point, view the YouTube video by searching "basketball moonwalking bear." A wonderful video from the UK with the goal of making cycling safer.

Welcome Jim Cain!

17. THE GATHERING PLACE

One goal of icebreakers in general is to help participants feel welcome. If you visit any airport, you'll see families, friends, and colleagues meeting and greeting each other in warm and wonderful ways. The Gathering Place is a technique for helping participants quickly find their place. To make things even easier, prepare signs with the subject matter, topic, or focus of each group in advance.

For example, if you want to invite lunchtime conversations between conference participants, you can place signs at each table designating topics of interest to the group, and allow participants to self-select which table they will occupy. Or, if you want to organize your summer camp staff by program area, you can add a number, letter, symbol, or color to their nametag, and then have your group leaders hold up signs with the same designation.

But since this activity was inspired during an international flight arrival in the UK, perhaps the best way to make your participants feel welcome is to greet every one of them (and their luggage) exactly as you would do in an airport. Invite members of your staff to create large, colorful signs (or banners) with the name of the person they are meeting, and hold them up as they arrive. Your participants will feel like rock stars and know exactly where to go.

I once flew to Shannon, Ireland, on an overnight flight from the USA. I was a bit jet-lagged when I arrived, but I gathered my luggage and headed off for the arrivals area of the airport to meet the folks who would transport me to my workshop location. Some airports have an official meeting point designated with signs in the arrival hall, but the airport in Shannon, Ireland airport went one step further. In the arrivals hall, there was a desk with dozens of markers and bright pink signs printed with the phrase, "I am looking for _____"

Those meeting passengers were free to create a sign with the name of the person they were meeting, but a few creative folks had written other catchy phrases, such as: "I am looking for the Holy Grail," "I am looking for the tallest man in Ireland," "I am looking for the smartest woman in all of Europe," etc. One enterprising lad had even glued a photograph of the passenger he was meeting onto the cardboard sign.

Nowadays, international airline passengers are met by limo drivers with computer tablet images of their name, spelled out in neat black text on a white screen. But I still prefer the creative signs I witnessed in Ireland (and I still have one!)

Doodles

Complete each illustration by drawing, writing, sketching, scribbling, or doodling something in each square.

18. DOODLES

You are welcome to make photocopies of the ready-to-copy Doodles page. Pass out a page of these Doodles to each person in your group, and invite them to finish each illustration. When each person in your group has completed this task, read the following information and discuss the question at the end of each commentary.

Square #1: Imagination

> "Imagination is more important than knowledge."
>
> —Albert Einstein

> "Use your imagination not to scare yourself to death but to inspire yourself to life."
>
> —Adele Brookman

> "To invent, you need a good imagination and a pile of junk."
>
> —Thomas A. Edison

This block illustrates how you use your imagination. If you draw numbers here, you have a mathematical imagination. If you draw objects, such as a golf flag, sailboat, or kite, you are inventive. If you draw natural objects, such as a tree, you enjoy nature in your world. Question: What have you dreamed of that has yet to become reality?

Square #2: Foundation

> "If you have built castles in the air, your work need not be lost; that is where they should be. Now put the foundations under them."
>
> —Henry David Thoreau

This block illustrates your foundation or support system in life. If you draw a house or barn, you have a classic foundation based on structure. If you draw irregular geometric patterns or objects, your foundation is often chaotic and changing. If you draw people or faces, you pull support from other people in your life. Question: Who can you depend upon for support?

Square #3: Creativity

> *"Creativity is the power to connect the seemingly unconnected."*
>
> —William Plomer

> *"Don't think. Thinking is the enemy of creativity
> It's self-conscious, and anything self-conscious is lousy.
> You can't try to do things. You simply must do things."*
>
> —Ray Bradbury

This block gives insight to your creative process. If you draw simple shapes with minimal lines, your creative process is simple and straightforward. If you draw multi-line patterns or complicated illustrations, you are a complex thinker and probably know how to program your DVR or create your own app or web page. Question: What have you invented or thought about inventing?

Square #4: Self-Image

> *One of the multiple intelligences defined by Howard Garner.*

This block is how you see yourself. If you draw a face, it is your own self-image! If you draw objects, those objects speak of what you believe defines your life. A clock denotes attention to the passing of time. A pizza, awareness of food. A coin, financial concerns. A ball, spiral, balloon, or target, playfulness. Question: Name one thing that you can do really well.

Square #5: Hopes, Dreams, & Aspirations

> *"The biggest adventure you can ever take
> is to live the life of your dreams."*
>
> —Oprah Winfrey

This block reveals your hopes, dreams, and aspirations. If you draw something vertical, such as a ladder, rocket ship, tall building, or tree, you have high hopes. If you draw something like a fence or doorway, you see barriers to moving forward. If you draw natural objects, such as a tree or flower, you dream of wide-open spaces. Question: What is a goal you have set for yourself to accomplish in the next five years? Ten years? Twenty years?

Square #6: What's on Your Mind?

What would you write here as your personal quotation?

—You

This final block is your personal statement. It reveals a word or message that you find important. Hello and Hi are both common, but other words often appear. If you draw only outside the thought balloon, you are a maverick and like to play without rules. If you draw in bold letters, you are confident in public. If you combined words and pictures, you are comfortable expressing yourself. Question: If you could have any bumper sticker on your car, what would it say?

In addition to the Doodles shown here, there are now dozens of books filled with doodling opportunities, including: *Doodle All Year* by Taro Gomi, *Do You Doodle?* by Nikalas Catlow, *Terry Denton's Bumper Book of Silly Stuff To Do,* and *Oodles of Doodles* by Nikalas Catlow. You can also find hundreds of coloring books (for kids and adults) and (my favorite) *Zentangles* (a pattern-making meditation) in such books as: *Zentangle Basics* by Suzanne McNeill and *Totally Tangled* by Sandy Steen Bartholomew.

I feel compelled to inform you that there is absolutely no scientific data connecting your drawings here to any of the six characteristics I've mentioned above. This is simply a playful way to discuss some interesting details of both art and human nature. Have fun, and don't take the answers or yourself too seriously.

19. GROUP PHOTOGRAPHS

Wouldn't it be great if a photograph had been taken during the signing of the Declaration of Independence? Illustrations and sketches, perhaps even a painting or two, but a true photograph would be historically amazing.

It can be difficult for people to realize when they are in an epic situation. Often this realization doesn't occur until long after the event is past. Over 100 years ago, Sir Ernest Shackleton sailed his crew to Antarctica on a ship named The Endurance. The story of their journey was indeed epic, and the photographs (and movies) produced by photographer Frank Hurley are historically significant.

Imagine what your group will experience when you share photographs of your time together with them a week or two after the event. And don't forget to include the photographer in your photograph collection. Frank Hurley's photograph of the crew of the Endurance (including one stow-away) was missing one essential member of the crew: Hurley himself.

With the variety of social media available today, sharing photographs from your group experiences is an easy and fun way to remember the event long after it is over.

The Ohio State Conservation Camp was held at 4-H Camp Ohio each summer. A commercial photographer arrived at camp each year to take a photograph of the participants and staff. One year, the weather did not cooperate. Just as the group gathered on a grassy hillside, it began to rain. By the time everyone was inside, we were all soaking wet. An hour later, the rain stopped, people had changed clothes, and we tried again. Sure enough, just as the photographer produced his large format box camera and tripod, it began to rain again. The camp director Denny Elliott asked the photographer, "Can you take a photograph in the rain?" "No problem," came the reply. That photograph is one of my favorite moments in film history. A watery blur of rain poured down on us, as we smiled from ear to ear.

A few days after ice crushed the Endurance in October 1915, photographer Frank Hurley stripped to the waist and dove underwater in the frigid Antarctic waters to recover several hundred glass photographic plates that were stored in the galley of the ship. The photograph of the crew (taken on September 1, 1915) is one that Hurley saved. You can find many photographs from this expedition online and in the book *South With Endurance: Shackleton's Antarctic Expedition 1914–1917, The Photographs of Frank Hurley*, taken from the archives of the Royal Geographical Society in London, the State Library of New South Wales in Sydney, and the Scott Polar Research Institute in Cambridge.

20. FORTUNE COOKIES

Chinese Fortune Cookies can become a new prop for your icebreaker activities, with just a few modifications. First, you'll need to obtain enough fortune cookies for your next group. If you get the edible variety, you can pull out the fortunes that come with each cookie, and replace them with printed icebreaker questions. Then, when your participants arrive, invite them to find a partner, enjoy their cookie, and ask their partner the question found inside. If you decide to use (and re-use) the fabric variety of fortune cookies, you can place an icebreaker question inside (and perhaps a piece of candy, too).

The fortune cookie technique mentioned here is actually a kind of random number generator for icebreaker conversation. Participants randomly choose a fortune cookie and then discuss the question inside. You can also use this technique for the final debriefing session in your group experience. Instead of opening icebreaker questions, fill your fortune cookies with questions for reviewing and reflection. You can find many more processing, debriefing, reviewing, and reflection activities in the book *A Teachable Moment* (ISBN 978-0-7575-1782-2) by Jim Cain, Michelle Cummings, and Jennifer Stanchfield, available from www.healthylearning.com and www.training-wheels.com.

You can purchase a collection of fabric fortune cookies from www.training-wheels.com or create your own with instructions available on the Internet. There are dozens of craft (and cooking) websites with information on how to make your own fabric (and edible) fortune cookies.

Did you know that the fortune cookie is an American invention? The San Francisco bakery Benkyodo is credited with the creation of a cookie which features a piece of paper on which a prophecy or aphorism is written.

In Japanese temples, a different form of fortune is available. By making a donation and then randomly shaking loose a numbered stick from a sealed box, an omikuji fortune is revealed.

21. THAT PERSON OVER THERE

Here is a brilliant technique for learning the names of people in your group, especially when business cards or removable nametags are available.

Invite your audience to hold their nametag in one hand. For Round One, ask everyone to find a partner and introduce themselves. At the end of the introduction, partners switch nametags.

In Round Two (and beyond), each person introduces themselves when meeting a new partner, but then also produces the nametag they are holding and points out this person to their new partner as well. "Hi, I am Jim. But that person over there [pointing] is Kirk." At the end of conversation, partners again switch nametags, and the activity continues.

After five or six exchanges, the facilitator halts the game and invites everyone to return the nametag they are holding to the original owner (introducing themselves when they do). Then play this game again, and encourage your audience to meet new people this time.

If you don't happen to have business cards or nametags available for this activity, you can still play by having everyone write their first and last name on an index card. Then you can re-use these same index cards for the activities Do You Like Your Neighbor? or Have You Ever?

Here is yet another great activity from Chris Cavert. Chris's latest book is *Portable Teambuilding Activities: Games, Initiatives and Team Challenges for Any Space* (ISBN 978-1-9390-1914-1), available from www.wnbpub.com and www.healthylearning.com.

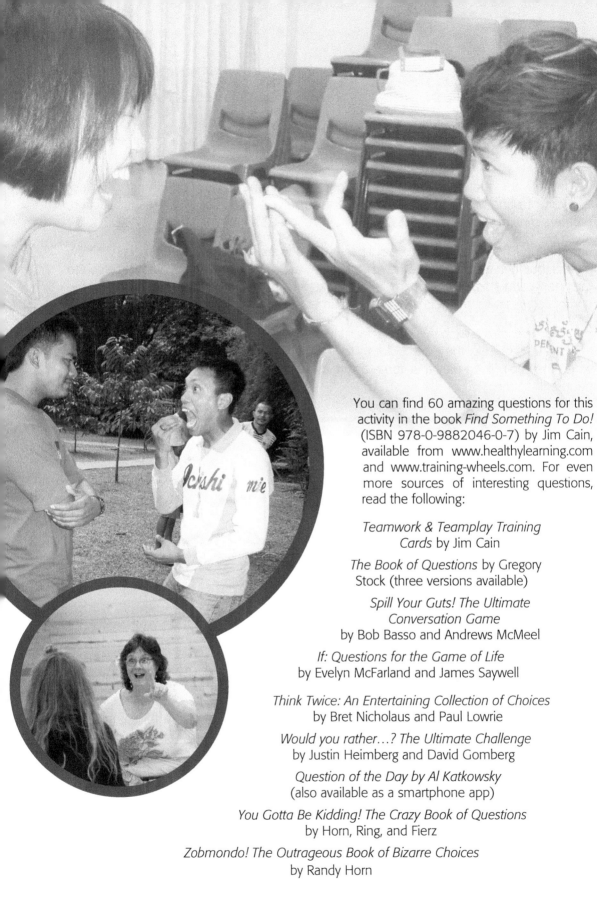

You can find 60 amazing questions for this activity in the book *Find Something To Do!* (ISBN 978-0-9882046-0-7) by Jim Cain, available from www.healthylearning.com and www.training-wheels.com. For even more sources of interesting questions, read the following:

Teamwork & Teamplay Training Cards by Jim Cain

The Book of Questions by Gregory Stock (three versions available)

Spill Your Guts! The Ultimate Conversation Game by Bob Basso and Andrews McMeel

If: Questions for the Game of Life by Evelyn McFarland and James Saywell

Think Twice: An Entertaining Collection of Choices by Bret Nicholaus and Paul Lowrie

Would you rather…? The Ultimate Challenge by Justin Heimberg and David Gomberg

Question of the Day by Al Katkowsky (also available as a smartphone app)

You Gotta Be Kidding! The Crazy Book of Questions by Horn, Ring, and Fierz

Zobmondo! The Outrageous Book of Bizarre Choices by Randy Horn

22. CONCENTRIC CIRCLES

Invite everyone in your audience to find a partner and then form a double circle. One partner will have their back to the center of the circle. This is the inside circle. Their partner will stand facing them, with their back to the outside. This is the outer circle.

Next, the facilitator asks an icebreaking question for partners to discuss. For example, "Who was your favorite childhood friend?" Both partners answer this question. Next, the facilitator will ask members of one circle to rotate to a new position. For example, everyone in the outer circle rotate three people to the left. Then a new question is presented to the group, and the activity continues.

You'll want to have a collection of great questions to ask during each round of this activity. For example:

Discuss the last movie you saw and why it was good or bad. I'd like you to sum up your entire life in just five words. Tell me about the last time you were really surprised? What is the best meal you have ever eaten?

When you ask the members of your audience to find a partner and make a circle, it is common that people tend to select someone they know as their partner. Concentric Circles is an excellent way to encourage conversation between random people. Each time the facilitator rotates the circle, everyone in the audience has the opportunity to talk with a new partner.

The "elevator speech" is a brief (20 to 30 seconds long) message that you deliver quickly to your audience. It is approximately the length of time that it takes an elevator to arrive at the floor of choice. For example, when someone on an elevator asks you, "So, what do you do?" you have about 20 seconds to formulate and deliver your message before the elevator doors open and the passengers depart. This style of communication demands a very clear and concise reply. In the game of Concentric Circles, allow a few seconds after the question is presented for both partners to think about their responses before they begin talking.

Another variety of Concentric Circles is more recently known as Speed Dating. Participants are invited to a gathering where they have the opportunity to meet and greet other participants in a very time-controlled manner. Partners typically have only a few minutes each to talk to each other before moving on to new partners. Then, after meeting everyone in the room, participants decide who they would like to meet again, and who would like to meet them. Icebreakers for busy people.

The staff of Mexico Verde—a white water rafting and adventure resort near Veracruz, Mexico—told me a unique story about a small town near their resort. For over a hundred years, every Saturday evening at sunset, the unmarried men of the town walk counterclockwise around the town square, and the unmarried women walk clockwise. A historically significant version of speed dating that has been going on for decades.

23. SMARTPHONE ACTIVITIES

Chances are good that a majority of your audience have their mobile phones nearby, so let's use them for these get-acquainted activities. I've broken these mobile phone activities into three levels. Level One involves activities that you can share without disclosing any personal facts. Level Two activities include some social media and other public disclosures. Level Three activities include some that share personal or private information.

For Level One, invite partners (with their mobile phones) to share any of the following information: favorite music, most recently downloaded music or video, favorite games, recommendations for a favorite app, which app do they use the most, etc.

For Level Two, partners can share any of the following: current status of their social media page, books they are currently reading or listening to, five recent photos from their phone, what the current weather forecast is for where they live, which things take up the most memory on their smart phone.

For Level Three, some increasingly personal information includes: Most recent texts from their BFF, who is listed as their ICE (In Case of Emergency) contact on their mobile device, what does a Google Earth photo of their house look like, play a few seconds of their current favorite song, what was the last message they texted a member of their family, what is currently on their personal to-do list, and my favorite, if a picture is worth a thousand words, which photo on their mobile device is worth a thousand words? See the opposite page for one of my favorite photos and the story that goes with it.

A few of my favorite books filled with technological icebreakers include:

Team-Building Activities for the Digital Age: Using Activities to Develop Effective Groups by Brent Wolfe and Colbey Sparkman ISBN 978-0-7360-7992-1

50 Digital Team-Building Games: Fast, Fun Meeting Openers, Group Activities, and Adventures Using Social Media, Smart Phones, GPS, Tablets, and More by John Chen ISBN 978-1-1181-8093-8

If you were to look at the photos on my mobile phone, you would find amongst the many I have of my trip to Mongolia one that shows a large pan filled with roast meat and vegetables. After several days of training summer camp staffs in Mongolia, I was invited to visit one Mongolian camp. About 4 p.m. that day, the camp staff began bringing out a tasty variety of local foods. At 5 p.m., after an hour of eating, I was stuffed to capacity. At this point, some of the staff brought out the pan of roasted meat and placed the largest piece of meat on my plate. I turned to my translator and said, "You have to help me. I don't like to waste food, and I am so full I cannot eat another bite." At which point my translator said, "You don't understand. As the honored guest today, your job is feed everyone else at the table.' What a nice tradition, I thought, as I began carving up the meat and serving everyone gathered together. A nice tradition, indeed.

The communication activity Build It requires one team to construct a building block structure and another team to replicate this structure without actually seeing it. Once, I placed each group in a separate room, but allowed them to talk to each other through an open door. At the end of exercise, the two structures were absolutely identical. The best I had ever seen. At this point, one person confided in me that they had used their mobile phones to send photographs of each structure to the team members in the other room. A valuable use of available technology!

During my first visit to Singapore, my friend Mike Lim of Innotrek invited me to present a workshop for his staff and several local trainers. I noticed during the training that every time I gave the group a break, they immediately pulled out their mobile phones and began tapping away at the screens. I thought perhaps they were texting friends, but I quickly discovered that they were taking notes. Electronic notes on their mobile phones. It seems that these versatile devices have even replaced pen and paper!

On a recent trip, I found myself in the Charlotte, North Carolina, airport between flights. As I sat in the departure area, I counted 18 people sitting nearby. Every single one of them was sitting alone, separate from anyone else, interacting with some form of smartphone, tablet, or laptop computer. They were connecting, just in an electronic way. Which reminds me what a colleague once told me about mobile phones: they make people far away seem close and people close by seem far away. Since smartphones are now an essential part of our culture, it is probably a good time to figure out how to use them to build unity, community, and connection, before we lose the opportunity all together.

24. WHAT IS IN YOUR POCKET?

Many of us carry essential stuff around with us—cell phone, wallet, credit cards, driver's license, coins, cash, maybe a few cherished photographs, etc. No doubt your participants have some of these essential things on them during your event, so why not use them as conversation starters?

First, invite your audience to form smaller groups of about six people. Next, ask for a volunteer in each group to share some of the (non-monetary) objects in their pocket (or wallet or purse). Some of us carry around some weird and yet memorable things, like movie ticket stubs from 11 years ago, or our lucky nickel, or a photograph with friends, or a newspaper article of importance, or receipts. See if anyone in your group can produce any of the following things from their pockets or wallet or purse:

> *a postage stamp, foreign currency, chewing gum, more than $1 worth of coins, a black-and-white photograph, business cards, candy, a crayon, a comb or brush, a map, two forms of identification, any kind of gift card, an automobile association (AAA) card, reading glasses, something belonging to someone else, a book, a postcard, a pen or pencil, jewelry, cosmetics, spare shoelaces, nail polish, something broken, a battery, a water bottle, a screwdriver, a toy animal, a raincoat or umbrella, food, a wrench, a toothbrush, a photograph or picture of a cartoon character, a paperclip, a rubber band, a flash drive, anything liquid, a bell, a tape measure or ruler, a key ring with more than 10 keys, a marble, duct tape, a stuffed animal, an index card, a flashlight, a fork or spoon, a plastic bag, sunglasses, a magnet, a rock.*

The second way to play this game is as a scavenger hunt—this time with multiple groups of about six people and one person designated as "runner" for each group. A facilitator or leader calls out any of the above objects, and the first runner to arrive next to the facilitator with that object wins two points, and any runner arriving after that, one point. The first group to reach 15 points wins.

If you like stories about the stuff people collect and the adventures they have, here are three of my favorite books about stuff. *One Red Paperclip* by Kyle MacDonald is the story of a guy who began with a single red paperclip and bartered and traded his way all the way up to a house! This event is basically the origin of the game, Bigger-Better-Heavier. Next is the book *A Life Sold: Whatever Happened to That Guy Who Sold His Whole Life on eBay* by Ian Usher. And finally in the book *Significant Objects*, Rob Walker and Joshua Glenn sell $129 worth of stuff for over $3,000 on eBay, after inventing stories of significance for each object. They sold the kinds of things some folks carry around in their pockets!

25. FOUR CORNERS

Four Corners is a great game for 20 or more players. Use masking tape or two ropes to create a large cross on the floor, dividing your available space into four quadrants. Next, have a ready list of categories for your audience to choose during the game. For example, if the category is transportation, you might identify each of the four quadrants as: sports car, SUV, pickup truck, or minivan. Then invite the members of your audience to stand in the quadrant that best suits their individual choice of transportation. Once they have gathered together in each quadrant, invite participants to share some of the things they like best about their choice.

For each successive round, include a question or an activity for each small group to complete during their time together. For example, if sports is the category, and football, baseball, basketball, and soccer are the choices, have each group come up with a cheer for that sport. If vacation locations is the category and beach, big city, mountains, or foreign country are the choices, invite each group to discuss what they would typically bring along with them for each location. If food is the category, you could list hamburgers, chicken, hotdogs, or salad as the choices, but you could also get a little more creative and list couscous, jicama, pad thai, or sashimi as the choices. Then have members of each group tell where they were when they first tried any of these foods. If music is the category, invite each quadrant to sing part of a song from their choice of music (such as rap, country, folk, rock, Top 40, etc.).

Instead of a four-quadrant playing field for this activity, consider the variation known as The Bus. Participants stand in the middle space between two rope lines (the bus). Each time the bus stops, group members make a choice and depart the bus on the left or right side. First stop: ice cream. Chocolate on the left, vanilla on the right. Next, invite participants to discuss the last time they had this flavor and the location. Then, back on the bus. Next stop: adventure travel. Sky diving to the left, deep sea diving to the right.

You can find this activity and many more in the book *Essential Staff Training Activities* (ISBN 978-0-7575-6167-2) by Jim Cain, Clare Marie Hannon, and David Knobbe, available from www.kendallhunt.com and www.healthylearning.com.

The Statistical Treasure Hunt

A Mathematical Group Discovery Activity

The challenge of this activity is to add up the total score for each item below for every member of your group. Then compare your group's score with the score of other groups. Take time during the completion of this activity to discuss some of these quantities with the other members of your group.

- Total number of lottery tickets you have ever bought
- The average number of books you read each year
- The number of friends you have on social media
- The number of brothers and sisters you have
- The number of countries you have visited
- The number of languages you can speak
- Your height in inches (or cm)
- The number of pets you own

Total Score = _____

26. STATISTICAL TREASURE HUNT

Here is one of the few icebreakers I know that incorporates mathematics. Present each small group with a copy of the Statistical Treasure Hunt page. Instruct them to add up the total score for each item on the list for every member of their group.

Encourage each group to take time during the completion of this activity to discuss some of these quantities with the other members of their group. For example, when discussing how many siblings there are, which group member has the most? Or, do any of the various siblings in the group have the same name?

If you elect to create your own statistical treasure hunt sheet, be sure to include categories that are specific to the age, industry, or interests of your participants.

100 Activities That Build Unity, Community & Connection • Jim Cain

First Impressions

Form a group of three with two other participants that you do not know very well (yet), and have a seat. Within this group, you are to guess the following traits about your partners. This is not a conversation; just make your best guess, and write your answer in the outer spaces. When each of the three participants in your group has finished, begin sharing both your guesses, and then the true information about each trait with each other. How many answers did you guess correctly?

Person on your left side			Person on your right side	
Your Guess	**The True Info**	**Traits**	**The True Info**	**Your Guess**
		Where were they raised (farm, city, suburbs, etc.)?		
		What would be a perfect gift for them?		
		What is their favorite food?		
		What type of music do they listen to (rock, country, folk, hip-hop, classical, etc.)?		
		What is most difficult about their job?		
		What do you have in common with this person?		

100 Activities That Build Unity, Community & Connection • Jim Cain

27. FIRST IMPRESSIONS

Make a photocopy of the First Impression activity page for each person in your group. Then invite everyone in your audience to create a group of three and have a seat. Encourage groups to form with three people that do not know each other well. The first part of this activity is basically a guessing game, not a conversation. Players in each small group consider each of the topics listed in the middle of the page and guess what they believe are the correct choices for each of their two partners. When everyone in the group is finished writing down their guesses, players share what they have written and then find out the truth for each person. Players keep track of how many times they guess correctly and incorrectly, continuing to share until all six topics have been discussed.

100 Activities That Build Unity, Community & Connection • Jim Cain

Autographs

First, write your first name in the block to the right. Then find another person who **has done** (sign the top portion of the block) or **has not done** (sign the bottom portion of the block) any of the activities listed below. You can sign a *maximum of two blocks* on anyone's autograph page.

Hello, my name is:

Your first name here, in great big letters.

I have done this signature

**Example:
Has gone water skiing**

I have not done this signature

- Knows someone famous
- Has an unusual hobby
- Knows how to program a DVR
- Has been to Mount Rushmore
- Has ridden a camel or unicycle
- Had an unusual job
- Has many siblings
- Collects something interesting
- Plays a musical instrument
- Can speak a foreign language
- Likes their dentist
- Looks the most like you
- Works as hard as you do
- Would bungie jump if the opportunity occurred
- Has performed on stage
- Has been to summer camp
- Has been on TV

www.teamworkandteamplay.com

100 Activities That Build Unity, Community & Connection • Jim Cain

28. AUTOGRAPHS

Collecting signatures (autographs) is a classic icebreaking activity. You might remember an earlier version of this activity called Name Bingo. On the opposite page, you will find my favorite version of this activity. In this version, every person you meet becomes important because they can either answer yes or no to any topic on the page. For example, if the topic is "Plays a Musical Instrument," if the answer is yes, sign your name in the top space of each block, or if the answer is no, sign your name in the bottom space of the block. Either way, you can collect a signature from every person you meet.

Feel free to make copies of this page for everyone in your audience, and encourage each person to write their name clearly in the space provided in the upper right corner of the page. Then invite them to mingle and find people to sign each block on the page.

In my training programs, I like to use what I call the TGR model for group dynamics. TGR stands for Task, Growth, and Relationships—the three ingredients that I believe make up a high performing work group or team. In the game of Autographs, participants are typically focused on gathering autographs and filling in all the blocks on their sheet of paper. Halfway through this activity, I typically stop the group, share the TGR model, and then invite them to continue, but focus less on completing the task (filling their sheet with signatures) and more on the relationship component (hearing the story behind the signature). On the sheet for example, there is a question that states, "Have you every ridden a camel or unicycle?" For those that have, you know there must be a story behind that event. Find out what it is.

Hieroglyphics
A Linguistic Challenge for Groups

Decode each of the cryptic messages below, and write the true message near it.
For example, message L below decodes as "a little bit more."

A.   GESG

B.   Traveling
      CCCCCCC

C.   2 UM + 2 UM

D.   TIMING   TIM ING

E.   HIJKLMNO

F.   YOU/JUST/ME

G.   EILN PU

H.   Often, Often, Often, Not, Not

I.   T   I   M   E
     abdefgh

J.   _____ it

K.   LOOK KOOL CROSSING

L.   bit MORE

M.   0, , 2, 3, 4, 5

N.    O E O (car image)

O.   L|AST

P.   • THAT'S

Q.   nafish   nafish

R.   TRN

S.   clo

T.   SOM

U.   SSSSSSSSSSC

V.   Wire
     Just

W.   BAN   ANA

X.   ME QUIT

Y.   SIGHT   LOVE
     SIGHT
     SIGHT

Z.   Wheather

100 Activities That Build Unity, Community & Connection • Jim Cain

29. HIEROGLYPHICS

Feel free to make copies of the word puzzles (Hieroglyphics) shown on the opposite page. You will need one copy of this page for each group of three people. Sharing resources is part of working together as a team. Allow each group of three to work on this challenge for about five minutes, and then encourage each small group to "double their brainpower" by combining with another nearby group (to form a group of six).

One of the teachable moments in this activity is realizing that none of us is as smart as all of us. If we work together, we can do anything!

One of the variations I like for this activity helps to reduce the competition that sometimes occurs when teams are working on a challenge with other teams nearby. After doubling the brainpower of each group of three, creating a group of six, I invite one person from each group of six to come together as ambassadors for their group. When the ambassadors gather together, they can discuss the word puzzles they have solved and look for help in the ones they still need to decode. After a minute or two, I send the ambassadors back to their groups and allow another minute or two to finish the activity, before sharing the answers below.

Here are the solutions to the hieroglyphics found on page 78.

A. Scrambled Eggs
B. Traveling Overseas (over C's)
C. Forum (4 UM)
D. Split Second Timing
E. H2O = Water (from H to O)
F. Just Between You and Me
G. Line Up (in Alphabetical Order)
H. More Often Than Not
I. Long Time – No See (no C)
J. Blanket = Blank It
K. Look Both Ways Before Crossing
L. A Little Bit More
M. No One (No 1)
N. Eraser (E racer)
O. Last But Not Least
P. That's Beside the Point
Q. Tuna Fish (two nafish)
R. No U-Turn
S. Partly Cloudy
T. The Start of Something Big
U. Tennessee (10S C)
V. Just Under the Wire
W. Banana Split
X. Quit Following Me
Y. Love at First Sight
Z. A Bad Spell of Weather

You will find this activity and 99 more in the book *Teambuilding Puzzles* (ISBN 978-0-7575-7040-7) by Mike Anderson, Jim Cain, Chris Cavert, and Tom Heck, available from www.kendallhunt.com and www.healthylearning.com.

30. COMMONALITIES

This activity has three levels. In Level One, two people attempt to find three things they have in common. Food, travel, music, books, sports, and families are often potential themes. After finding three commonalities, this group of two finds another ready group of two to form a group of four. In Level Two, these four must now find two things they have in common, and they cannot use any of the previous commonalities from Level One. When this group has identified two unique commonalities, they join another group of four and these eight people must find just one unique commonality to complete Level Three.

> Level One: 2 People – 3 Things in Common
>
> Level Two: 4 People – 2 Things in Common
>
> Level Three: 8 People – 1 Thing in Common

I typically like to mention that the more interesting the commonality, the better. Finding out that you and your partner both like ice cream is fairly common. Finding out that you and your partner both like the same flavor of ice cream is truly unique. Encourage your participants to find some truly unique commonalities with their partners. The more unusual the connection, the stronger the bond formed between the members of each group.

In addition to serving as an opening activity, Commonalities also helps organize your audience into circles of exactly eight people. If you like, you can flow from this activity right into one of the following using the circle formation: All My Life's a Circle, Core Groups, Boogie Ball, The Imaginary Obstacle Course, or the Story Stretch.

You can find this activity and many other no-prop activities in the book *Find Something to Do!* (ISBN 978-0-9882046-0-7) by Jim Cain, available from www.training-wheels.com and www.healthylearning.com.

31. FACE TO FACE / BACK TO BACK

Begin this activity by inviting your participants to find a partner and then stand back to back. Next, provide your audience with a suitable discussion topic, such as: the last movie you watched and why it was good or bad. Then say the phrase "Face to face," and instruct everyone to find a new partner and discuss the topic mentioned. After a minute or two (or when you hear the volume of conversation in the room dramatically decrease), shout "Back to back," and instruct everyone to stand back to back with their most recent discussion partner. Repeat for several rounds.

Discussion topics can include: best meal they have ever eaten, the farthest they have every traveled from home, their favorite class (or teacher) in school or college, their first vehicle, their family's funniest story, or the best birthday or holiday present they have ever received.

If, at any time in this activity, one of your participants finds themselves without a partner, invite them to raise both hands high in the air and wave their hands and fingers (the universal sign for *I am looking for a partner*). This technique makes it easy for individuals to be seen and find a partner. And, if you happen to have an odd number of participants, the group leader can join in.

For those group leaders that do not possess a loud voice, this activity provides a useful technique for reducing the noise level and getting the attention of your participants. By simply yelling "Back to back," most of the group will reposition themselves and quit talking, creating a quieter opportunity for the group leader to be heard.

Here are a few resources filled with interesting questions:

Teamwork & Teamplay Training Cards by Jim Cain

The Book of Questions by Gregory Stock (three versions available)

If: Questions for the Game of Life by Evelyn McFarland and James Saywell

Spill Your Guts! The Ultimate Conversation Game by Bob Basso and Andrews McMeel

Think Twice: An Entertaining Collection of Choices by Bret Nicholaus and Paul Lowrie

Would You Rather…? The Ultimate Challenge by Justin Heimberg and David Gomberg

Question of the Day by Al Katkowsky (also available as a smartphone app)

You Gotta Be Kidding! The Crazy Book of Questions by Randy Horn

32. THE WALK OF LIFE

Invite groups of three people to gather together, all facing the same direction. The person standing in the middle (center) of the trio is invited to share one significant event in their lives for each of 10 steps. As they move forward, their partners walk with them. After the 10th step, another member of the trio takes the middle position and heads off in a new direction as they share 10 significant events in their life, taking one step for each event mentioned.

As a variation of this activity, invite each person to share one significant event for every step the trio moves forward. This variation often creates more conversation between participants and is recommended especially if you think you might run out of time before each member of the group has shared their 10 significant events. If you are really pressed for time, you can reduce the number of significant events mentioned by each member of the trio from 10 to 5.

I created this activity during a CCI conference near Malaga, Spain. The basic idea was to share 10 significant events in your life—one event for every step you take. It is rather like another activity in this book, The Lifeline, but without the line. I initially thought about calling the activity 10 Steps, but a month after the CCI conference, I presented a workshop at the ACCT conference in Austin, Texas. One of my workshop participants (who facilitates activities in a prison environment) mentioned that he often uses a similar activity so that prisoners could share the path their life had taken, ultimately landing them in prison. He said this was a powerful but often heartbreaking recollection of their personal history. With his input and permission, I decided to rename the activity The Walk of Life, and it has had that name ever since.

Handshake Script

When I first began traveling to work with groups, I was invited to northern Canada. On my second day, a local from the area introduced himself and asked, "So, where are you from?" "How do you know I'm not from right here?" I said, to which he replied, "I don't think so. You don't sound the way we do up here. But if you want to blend in with the locals, I'll show you how we shake hands up here in the north country." He then proceeded to show me the lumberjack handshake.

One partner extends their right fist, thumbs up. The second partner makes a similar right-handed fist, grabbing their partners thumb, and placing their own thumb straight up. The first partner then adds their own left hand (in a similar fashion), followed by the second partners left hand. Next, these two partners saw back and forth, saying one of their names on the forward stroke, and the other on the backstroke ("Jim - Ted. Jim - Ted. Jim - Ted."

After shaking hands in this manner, turn to your partner and say, "I would never forget your face. I would always remember you in a crowd." Then hold up one, two, or three fingers. Go find a new partner with the same number of fingers showing.

After traveling in northern Canada, I then traveled out to Minneapolis, Minnesota. Now Minnesota is the Land of 10,000 Lakes. And the people of that area are largely of Norwegian heritage. So it is a pretty likely bet that when you meet a Minnesotan, they'll be both a Norwegian and a fisherman. And what kind of fisherman? Walleye, of course! So when you want to blend in with the locals in Minneapolis, here is a two-part handshake that you can use.

First, face your partner, throw both hands up in the air, and say, "Yahhh [your partner's first name]." Then reach out your hand (with your sleeves rolled up) and bypassing your partner's hand, slap your hand against their forearm (like the sound of a walleye slapping the bottom of the boat when you've landed a big one). Oh, I almost forgot, Norwegian walleye fishermen are mostly left handed, so be sure to try this particular handshake left-handed as well. Now turn to this partner and say, "See ya later, alligator." Then go find a new partner that feels the same way about broccoli that you do.

After visiting the Great Plains, I next traveled back to the state of Ohio. A very friendly state right there in the heartland of the country. Ohio is so friendly, it even has its own state handshake.

Face your partner, and together raise both hands above your head, fingers touching to make a large letter O, and say "O." Then shake hands and say "Hi." Finally, make another large letter O and again say "O." That's the Ohio handshake. Do it again!

Now say to your partner, "Don't go away, I'll be right back." Now find someone with the same color (or the same number) of eyes you have.

And finally, the New York [or the name of your local town here] coffee drinker's handshake. Face your partner and ask them about their favorite hot beverage in the morning. Place an imaginary cup of this hot beverage in your left hand. Be careful not to spill it. Raise your right hand to high-five your partner, miss, bend at the waist, lift the leg closest to your partner, and grasp their ankle with your hand and shake.

Now say to this partner, "Meet me right here in a minute."

Well, like all good education, if that was the lesson, here comes the test! Find your lumberjack partner and shake hands with them. (Some confusion occurs as everyone goes off to find their lumberjack partner. Plenty of sawing motion, and name shouting.) Then say, "Now your Norwegian Walleye fisherman partner." (Shouts of 'Yahh' are heard, and the sound of slapping.) Next, find your Buckeye partner. (Sounds of "O – hi – o" are heard.) And finally, find your coffee drinking partner.

33. HANDSHAKES

In the Western world, one of the most common forms of greeting is the handshake. But even this simple gesture has many regional variations. This activity not only invites your audience to get acquainted using some of these regional handshakes, but challenges your audience's short-term memory and facial-recognition capabilities.

You can use the script found on the opposite page to introduce four of my favorite novelty handshakes. After introducing all of these handshakes, invite the members of your audience to find their earlier partners and repeat the appropriate handshake with the appropriate partner.

For a number of years, I had the pleasure of working as a senior consultant to the Cornell Outdoor Education program. Dave Moriah has a long history with that program and was the first person I witnessed using novelty handshakes as group icebreakers. I've added a few new ones here, but Dave was the original inspiration.

34. ALL MY LIFE'S A CIRCLE

Invite groups of six participants to gather around a knotted Raccoon Circle that has been placed on the floor. The person nearest the knot tells some of the most interesting events of their life as they (and everyone in the group) slowly walk counterclockwise around the perimeter of the circle. When finished, another member of the group tells their story.

Some folks like to tell their entire life history in one revolution, while others may need several revolutions to complete their story. Either technique is acceptable. The power of this activity is to create an active, moving icebreaker and yet one that requires very little space for each group.

Almost any activity you can lead in a circle, you can modify or bend to facilitate it in a straight line. As an example, if you untie the knotted Raccoon Circle used in this activity, you can morph into another activity in this book: My Lifeline.

If you like to include music in the background during your programs, you might enjoy the song "Circle" on the Harry Chapin *Greatest Stories Live* album. I played this album over and over during my senior year at Youngstown State University.

A Raccoon Circle is a 15-foot (4.6 meter) long segment of 1-inch (25.4mm) wide tubular climbing webbing, available in many camping stores and occasionally in marine/hardware stores or horse tack shops. This webbing comes in a variety of colors and patterns and is extremely durable. For more Raccoon Circle activities, see *The Revised and Expanded Book of Raccoon Circles* (ISBN 978-0-7575-3265-8) by Jim Cain and Tom Smith, available from www.healthylearning.com and www.kendallhunt.com, and download a free PDF document filled with Raccoon Circle activities from www.teamworkandteamplay.com/resources.html.

35. CORE GROUPS

Occasionally at a conference or similar gathering, you may want to organize small groups and then reconvene these same groups at other times during the event. One of the easiest and most fun ways to do this is to introduce the concept of core groups. A core group is identified by two unique things: a hand signal (visual) and a sound (auditory).

Once you have formed small groups, invite each group to create their own unique hand signal and sound. Invite them to practice so that every member of their group can mimic these signals when asked. You might even ask for each group to demonstrate their movement and sound, just to make sure each group is truly unique. Next, invite everyone to individually mingle around the space available. After 30 seconds or so, yell "Core groups," and watch as everyone begins making hand signals and sounds, and ultimately gathering together with the other members of their core group.

Anytime you need to reconvene these smaller groups, just yell "Core groups," and your audience with have no trouble finding the other members of their group.

When I organize an hour-long session of icebreakers, I recommend spending about half the time in one big group and half the time in smaller, more intimate groups. This way, each person will have the opportunity to meet everybody a little, and some people a lot. It is not uncommon that folks know the members of their core group the best after a series of activities together.

36. MINGLE

Invite your audience to mingle about in the space available. As they randomly mix, shout out one of the following categories and instruct everyone to gather in small groups based upon one of the following criteria:

Hairstyle, type of shoes, shirt color, favorite ice cream, jewelry, family size, height

Once smaller groups have formed, provide them with interesting questions to discuss with the other members of their group. For example, "Where did you buy the shirt you are wearing today?" or "What flavor of ice cream is your favorite, and where can you buy it?"

Repeat this activity several times, using the criteria above, or by creating your own criteria for groups.

I've witnessed many facilitators and group leaders present their version of Mingle, but Elbert Hargrave of North Carolina was the first and possibly the best I've seen. Early in my career, Tom Heck, Elbert, and I co-facilitated a series of workshops for the Department of Juvenile Justice, and Mingle was used in every workshop to build unity, community, and connection with our participants.

During a corporate teambuilding workshop, I included Mingle as one of the opening activities and discovered that the manager of the group also enjoyed coconut ice cream. After our half-day program, I found a store that stocked coconut ice cream and showed up at Joyce's office with two pints of ice cream and two spoons. We reviewed the day's teambuilding program together, ate ice cream, and made plans for future programs. As fate would have it, that was the last time I would see Joyce, but I will always remember the smile on her face as we ate ice cream together.

You can find this activity and many other no prop activities in the book *Find Something to Do!* (ISBN 978-0-9882046-0-7) by Jim Cain, available from www.training-wheels.com and www.healthylearning.com.

37. CHANGE THREE THINGS

*Change isn't always better, but if you want
to get better, you have to change!*

This activity begins with partners facing each other and carefully observing the details of their partner's features and appearance. After a minute or two of observation, invite partners to stand back to back, and then alter three things about their appearance. When both partners have completed these changes, they stand face to face and see if they can each identify what is now different about their partner.

After the initial round changing three things, try this activity again, but this time encourage your participants to change five things about themselves. In Round Three, you might even suggest changing seven things. In each round, when participants go back to back, they are facing many others in the room, who often are sources for making changes (such as trading shoes, or borrowing a hat or jewelry). There are people around you, who care about you, that can help you when you need to make a change in your life.

This is just one of the activities in this book that explores some of the parameters of social and emotional intelligence.

Something Is Different

For larger groups of about 20 people, try this second version of Change Three Things. Invite a volunteer to walk slowly around and then exit the room. While outside the room, this person changes three things about their appearance. Then they return, the group (silently) tries to identify all three of the things that are now different. When someone thinks they have all three changes identified, they share their guesses out loud.

The Big Answer

We all have questions, for which we are constantly looking for answers. Write your choice of question in the space below, and let's see if we can help you generate some appropriate answers, or at least some food for thought.

My question is:

For those of you receiving this page, your task is to carefully consider the question above, and write your best advice, answer, or comment in one of the spaces below.

38. THE BIG ANSWER

Here is a very simple way for team members to solicit advice from other participants. You are welcome to make photocopies of the opposite page for each member of your group. Then instruct your participants to write one of their current challenges in the space provided (one question or challenge per page).

At this point, there are several ways to complete this activity. First, if participants are seated at a table, invite them to pass their Big Answer document one person to their right, and continue this process until everyone has seen and written some advice on each page. A second method is to place all the Big Answer documents on a table or wall and allow participants to read and write their recommendations throughout the day, during breaks. A final technique is to have participants mingle, trading papers each time they meet a new person, and writing their own comments whenever appropriate.

For a number of years, I've been using The Big Question as one of my favorite icebreakers. During a corporate teambuilding event, one manager remarked "We already have enough big questions; what we need are big answers!" So, after lunch that day, I created a document (very much like the one shown on the opposite page) and shared it with the group. That day, everybody went home with some suggestions and recommendations on how to solve their biggest challenges at work, and now, you can too.

The Big Answer was originally published in the book *Essential Staff Training Activities* (ISBN 978-0-7575-6167-2) by Jim Cain, Clare Marie Hannon, and David Knobbe, and is available from www.kendallhunt.com and www.healthylearning.com.

39. KERFUFFLE

Kerfuffle : A commotion or fuss, confusion, disorder

Hullabaloo: An uproar, clamor, brouhaha, pandemonium, mayhem

Hurly Burly: A busy, boisterous activity

This high-energy activity has had many names over the years. I like the name Kerfuffle, but feel free to call the game anything you like.

Begin with a collection of index or playing cards, and write one of the tasks (found on the following pages) with permanent marker on each card. This is a perfect activity if you happen to have a few decks of incomplete (or complete!) playing cards lying around the house. If not, index cards work just fine.

Next, assemble about twice as many cards as you have participants. Gather your group together, and toss the entire deck of cards into the air (so that they randomly float down to the floor). Then instruct each person to pick up a card and perform the task written there. Once they have completed the task, place that card on a chair in the center of the room and then choose another card.

The uproar in the room will be substantial as participants perform the various tasks written on the cards. This is a perfect activity for creating five minutes of boisterous activity between presentations or after a long period of audience inactivity.

I have chosen many of the tasks in my deck of Kerfuffle cards to require interaction with other participants in the group. This version creates substantial mayhem and also provides for an interesting teachable moment—namely, when you received your task card, did you complete your task first or help someone else complete the task on their card first?

Make Your Own Kerfuffle Cards

Here are 65 tasks that you can use to make your own Kerfuffle cards.

> Skip around the room with a partner.
> Line up five people tallest to shortest.
> Get three people to laugh very loud with you.
> Do 10 push-ups, or get 10 people to each do one push-up.
> Build a living Mt. Rushmore with four people; take a selfie.
> Sing your favorite song. All of it!
> Get four people to whistle a happy tune.
> See if you can get everyone to clap at the same time.
> Make racecar sounds as you drive one lap around the group.
> Get five people to each make a different farmyard animal sound.
>
> Get five people to each make a different wild animal sound.
> Pretend to ice skate with a partner.
> Pretend to roller skate with a partner.
> Invent a new style of ballroom dance with a partner.
> Conduct an orchestra with as many people as you can playing imaginary instruments.
> Wave both hands, and yell "Yoo-hoo!"
> Secretly follow another person around the room for one minute.
> Organize eight people to sit or kneel in a circle.
> Get five people to say 'Shhhhh!' together
> Get four people to each do one letter of YMCA.
>
> Waltz with a partner.
> Get several people to stomp loudly around the room.
> Get four people to sing the alphabet song: "A, B, C, D, E, F, G …"
> Trade cards with another person.
> Shake hands with four people, then yell "Yahoo!"
> Find your closest twin, and take a selfie with them.
> Pretend to cry until someone asks you why you are crying.
> Stare into someone's eyes for 20 seconds.
> Run five circles around a single person.
> If anyone approaches you, run away.
>
> Dance wildly until someone smiles at you.
> Talk-talk, double-double
> Form a line of people, and do the bunny hop for one minute.
> Walk like a robot through the middle of the group, twice.
> When someone approaches you, put your hand to your ear and ask, "Do you hear that?"

Point to the ceiling (or sky) and say, "Well look at that" until someone else looks up.
Stand really, really close to someone for one minute.
Get as many people as you can to sing "Happy Birthday to you."
Collect as many shoes as you can, and make a tower from them.
Moo like a cow until someone moos with you.
Find the tallest person in the room, and greet them with "Howdy!"
Pretend to jump rope solo, and then with two other people holding the rope.
Dribble an imaginary basketball around the room.
Laugh as loud as you can for 10 seconds.
Swim around the room in backstroke, sidestroke, butterfly, and freestyle.

Row a boat all the way around the room.
Pretend to be a quarterback and yell "Blue 54, blue 54, hike, hike," and throw a pass.
Paddle a canoe all the way around the room.
Tell five people what your favorite food is.
Create a famous work of art, and keep at it until someone guesses what you are doing.
Ask someone to tie your shoelaces for you.
Listen for someone to moo, and then yell "Yee-haw!"
Flap your arms like you are flying for one minute. Then ask someone to join you.
Find three people whose watches (cell phones) all have a different time.
Find a person who is wearing the most jewelry, and high-five them.

Find a person who has the longest hair, and shake their hand.
Thumb-wrestle with two other people. Best of three wins.
Wink at every person who makes eye contact with you.
Strike a yoga pose while saying "Inner peace, inner peace …"
Close your eyes until someone asks if they can help you.
Shake hands with everyone in the room.
Count to 20 in any language you like.
Stand on one leg, and get five people to join you.
Get three more people to join your bobsled team, then circle the group.
Pretend to boldly juggle with a partner.

Over the years, I've heard this activity called by different names and from many different sources (see the *Cokesbury Stunt Book*, copyright 1934). But recently, several groups have reintroduced this activity under the name 52 Pickup. Project Adventure, High Five Learning Center, and Training Wheels all have card versions of this activity that are a riot to play and enjoy. If you visit www.high5adventure.org, you can even download a free version of 52 Pickup from their community blog page.

40. MIXER DANCES

Mixer dances are simple dances where couples change partners frequently. Here are two of my favorite ways to bring music and movement to your next opening activities event.

The Jiffy Mixer

This activity is the perfect first dance to share with your audience. The movements are simple, the music uncomplicated, and best of all, it's fun. Begin the dance in a large double circle with partners facing each other, holding hands. Begin with the inside partner's left foot (outside partner's right foot) heel, toe, heel, toe, slide, together, slide. Then reverse, the inside partner's right foot (outside partner's left foot) heel, toe, heel, toe, slide, together, slide. Then drop hands with partner, and jump backward (chug) about three inches, like this: chug, clap, chug, clap, chug, clap, chug, clap. Then angle to the right to find a new partner. Join hands. Repeat. ("Jiffy Mixer," by Pete Lofthouse Band, Windsor Records 4684)

White Silver Sands Mixer

This activity begins with couples standing side-by-side, facing counterclockwise around the circle, holding inside hands. Begin by walking forward four steps, then independently turning around (180 degrees) and backing up four steps. Then return by walking forward four steps, turning around and backing up four steps. Then step away from your partner (but don't let go), and when you are away, say "Away!" Then step together (and say "Together!"). Then repeat, "Away! Together!" And finally the insider partner drops hands with their partner, turns left over their shoulder, and takes a new partner one couple behind their last position, repeating the dance with a new partner. ("White Silver Sands Mixer" by Al Russ Orchestra, Grenn Recordings 4021, Choreography by Manning and Nita Smith)

My father, grandfather, and I are all square dance callers. So social dances have always been part of my repertoire of opening activities. For more information about using dancing as part of your next program, you can download the document "Building Community With Music, Singing, and Dance" at the T&T website: www.teamworkandteamplay.com/resources.html. You may also enjoy the book (and music CD), *Dance a While* by Jane Harris, Anne Pittman, and Marlys Waller.

At the International Camping Congress held in Antalya, Turkey, I was asked to organize an opening icebreaker session so that participants from over 30 countries could meet each other. Of course, language was a challenge, so rather than focus on activities with lots of speaking and little movement, I chose to use activities with plenty of movement and just a little conversation. Of all the activities I presented during that session, the two mixer dances (above) that I shared were the crowd favorites.

For more information about the International Camping Fellowship (ICF) and future International Camping Congresses, visit: www.campingfellowship.org

41. THE MORNING DANCE PARTY

The Morning Dance Party is a musical warm-up activity that incorporates leadership. Invite your audience to form one large circle. Then select an upbeat music selection that will inspire and motivate your audience. One person leads the circle by performing a simple dance movement, and everyone in the circle replicates this movement. After a few seconds, this first leader points to the person on their left and passes the leadership to them. Continue until everyone in the circle has had the opportunity to lead.

The length of most songs is sufficient for circles of about 30 people. If your group is larger than 30 people, I would recommend making multiple circles of 30 or fewer, so that everyone will have the opportunity to be a leader during this activity. If the song continues longer, some group members may have the opportunity to lead twice.

I was invited to train the staff of the YLCC summer leadership camp near Toronto, Canada. Just after breakfast, all the staff formed a large circle in the back of the dining hall. When I asked what was happening, Stu Saunders (the founder of YLCC) informed me that it was time for the morning dance party. As a very upbeat and inspirational song began playing, one person in the circle began leading a very simple dance movement and everyone in the circle replicated this movement. After a few seconds, the leader pointed to the person on their left, and the leadership passed to the next person in the circle, who began a different movement. This progression continues until everyone in the circle had the opportunity to be a leader at least once.

You can find The Morning Dance Party and 50 other activities, translated into 16 different languages in *The Teamwork & Teamplay International Edition* (ISBN 978-0-9882046-3-8), available from www.training-wheels.com and www.healthylearning.com.

42. THE IMAGINARY OBSTACLE COURSE

This no-prop activity integrates two valuable assets: imagination and a physical warm-up. Begin in small groups of eight people. A volunteer leads the entire group to the first element of an imaginary obstacle course. After describing and then demonstrating the proper technique for crossing their imaginary obstacle, all remaining members of the group follow their leader. Then another member of the group takes the leadership roll and leads the group through the next obstacle.

A variety of imaginary obstacles are possible. Climbing trees or infinite ladders, rope swings, swimming through giant waves in the ocean, jumping over ravines and crevasses, lifting heavy loads, juggling small animals, etc.

During one corporate teambuilding event in New York City, I used the Imaginary Obstacle Course as a morning warm-up activity. At one point, the vice-president of the group began doing log rolls across the carpeted floor. That was surprising, but what followed was even more surprising. Every member of his group followed him completely. When I asked the members of this group what would make them want to follow such a leader without reservation, they replied that this particular person had hired most of them, and they would follow him anywhere. If he asked them to do log rolls across the floor, then they would do log rolls across the floor. Even such a simple warm-up activity can demonstrate the power of effective leadership.

You can find this activity and many other no-prop activities in the book *Find Something to Do!* (ISBN 978-0-9882046-0-7) by Jim Cain, available from www.training-wheels.com and www.healthylearning.com.

43. BOOGIE BALL

Here is an outstanding musical warm-up activity will keep your audience moving. To begin, provide each group of eight people with a tennis ball, and instruct them to stand in a circle. Next, begin tossing the ball randomly around the circle. When music begins to play, the person currently holding the ball becomes the group leader and begins marching while the rest of the circle falls in line behind this leader. This continues (for about 20 seconds) until the music stops, at which time the group forms another circle and begins rapidly tossing the ball randomly to various people in the circle.

You can add a name game component to this activity if you like. In the first round, simply toss the ball randomly around the group and march behind the leader when the music plays. In rounds two and three, say your own name as you toss the ball, and chant the name of the leader as you follow them when the music plays. In rounds four and five, say the name of the person you are throwing the ball to and chant the name of the leader as you follow them around the room. These repetitions should help you learn and remember the names of the people in your group.

I like to use high-energy music for this activity. The higher the energy level of the music, the higher the energy level of the participants.

Chris Cavert shared this musical warm-up activity during a workshop we co-facilitated at the T.E.A.M. conference at N.E.I.U. in Chicago. You can read Chris's latest collection of teambuilding activities in his book *Portable Teambuilding Activities* (ISBN 978-1-939019-14-1) available from www.wnbpub.com. You can learn more about Chris, read his blog, and enjoy many more of his activities at www.fundoing.com.

44. THE METER

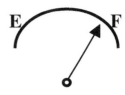

With a short piece of rope or a Raccoon Circle, make an arch shape like the one shown here. This is your fuel gauge, or any type of meter that you wish. Ask participants to stand outside the meter, at the position that best relates to them. For example, the amount of energy that you have right now could be just like a gas tank gauge (empty, half a tank, full).

This activity acquaints participants with each other, indicates preferences, and provides an opportunity to share some rather basic information about themselves without the need to justify or explain their decisions. This activity can also be used by a facilitator to gain immediate and useful information about their participants (for example: the number of hours spent working out each week, the number of books read in the past six months, the number of frequent flyer miles accumulated in the past year, the number of brothers and sisters in their family, or the number of hours of sleep they had last night).

For many choices in life, the answers are not simply black and white, yes or no, positive or negative, on or off. There are many that have plenty of gray space in between two extremes, or multiple possibilities, such as: the number of cups of coffee consumed every day, the number of miles driven to work each day, the number of people in their family, the number of books read each year from the library, or the number of things currently in their car trunk right now. The Meter is an interesting way for your participants to share information about themselves without ever having to speak.

A Raccoon Circle is a 15-foot (4.6 meter) long segment of 1-inch (25.4mm) wide tubular climbing webbing, available in many camping stores and occasionally in marine/hardware stores or horse tack shops. This webbing comes in a variety of colors and patterns. It is also one of the few teambuilding props that I have discovered that works fine when wet. So even the rain won't stop you from enjoying this activity.

For almost 200 Raccoon Circle activities see *The Revised and Expanded Book of Raccoon Circles* (ISBN 978-0-7575-3265-8) by Jim Cain and Tom Smith, available from www.healthylearning.com and www.kendallhunt.com, and download a free PDF document filled with Raccoon Circle activities from www.teamworkandteamplay.com/resources.html.

45. SUBWAY GREETINGS

Traveling by train, tram, subway, or bus in any part of the world can be spatially challenging, especially during the morning and evening commuting hours. Just visit any of these modes of transportation during a weekday, and you'll see for yourself. But this is exactly when you are most likely to see friends, colleagues, and business associates. So be prepared for greetings in small spaces with this handshake activity.

Begin by inviting your entire group to huddle closely together. Now instruct everyone to lock their feet in position. The goal is for everyone to twist, turn, and stretch so that they can shake hands (either hand is fine) with as many people as possible without moving their feet.

This activity provides everyone in your audience with the opportunity to stretch and greet several members of the group. Next, inform them that a significant number of people have departed the subway, leaving a bit more space. In this round, participants are again invited to shake hands, but are also allowed to move one of their feet, to reach even more members of the group. Their other foot may pivot (like a basketball player). Encourage everyone to stretch as far as they can to reach other members of the group. The goal in this round is to reach more even more people than were contacted in the first round.

While many facilitators use less debriefing with icebreakers and opening activities, there is an opportunity here for a unique teachable moment. In either the first or second round of this activity (with no moving feet, or just one), ask participants which of the following statements was truer:

> 1. That they disregarded the movement rules so that they could reach and connect with more members of the group.

> or

> 2. They followed the rules exactly, and thus limited the opportunity for reaching even more members of the group.

This is a great activity to use when you have severely limited space, such as in a conference room, tiny classroom, elevator, auditorium with fixed seating, or anytime movement is restricted because of the available space.

46. TRULY UNIQUE

You need New York, unique New York.
You know you need unique New York.

The goal of this activity is to celebrate the things in our history that make us truly unique in any group experience. And sometimes the things that make us unique are not unusual or even bizarre, but rather something simple (like being born in Ohio).

The first way to play Truly Unique is to invite everyone to write on an index card something they believe makes them truly unique. You are welcome to give examples, such as an unusual hobby or sport (I happen to throw boomerangs), playing an unusual musical instrument, speaking a unique foreign language, cooking or eating unusual foods, etc. Then collect the cards, shuffle them, and read aloud the various comments written there. Ask the group to guess which person each card refers to, but check to see if the comment is truly unique. That is, no one else in the group does that same thing.

A second way to play Truly Unique is to invite one person at a time to introduce themselves and mention something that they believe no one else in the group has ever experienced. If they are truly unique, the group gives them a standing ovation. If not, they are invited to try again, after everyone else has had a turn.

In the game *Have You Ever?* (activity number 13 in this book) a speaker introduces themselves and then discloses something that is true for them, such as "Have you ever been to a zoo?" At this point, everyone in the circle that has been to a zoo trades places with each other. Occasionally, a speaker may disclose something so unique that no one in the circle has experienced the same thing. This is an example of true uniqueness, something that no one else shares in the entire group. When this happens, I encourage everyone to give the speaker a standing ovation!

47. MINT CONDITION

While the various scenery, patterns, materials, words, and symbols vary on coins around the world, one feature that is fairly common is the date the coin was manufactured (minted). For your next icebreaker program, bring a handful of coins, and pass several of these coins to each small group of four to six people. Then ask each group to choose one coin, read the date, and then invite each person in the group to share one significant thing that happened in their life that year. Or each group can read the dates on all coins in their possession, and participants are free to choose any year they like when sharing something significant.

In the United States, paper money also has a date that you can use for this activity, but most bills are systematically retired when they become worn, so you are likely to only find dates from within the last 10 years or so.

Did you know that Mongolia does not currently use any coins as part of their currency system? The Mongolian Tughrik banknote is the only currency in that country and all notes feature a watermark of Chinggis Khaan (Genghis Khan). Coins in Mongolia are mostly collection items or tourist souvenirs.

48. FAVORITE SCAR STORIES

Almost no one gets through life without collecting a few scars along the way. And while this activity may not be appropriate for every group you facilitate, it can be a very powerful story experience when used properly. This is the type of activity that is improved when the facilitator is the first person to share. So, if you happen to have a scar or better yet a scar story, here is your opportunity to share it with your group.

> *On the last night of a 4-H leadership program at Camp Ohio, I was invited by a few friends to climb up to Vesper Hill and play my guitar. The sun had already set as I walked up through the darkened cabin area looking for my friends. At that time, Camp Ohio had wire clotheslines strung between cabins. I learned this fact a little too late. I walked straight into one of these lines, at nose height, in the darkness, and soon found myself flat on my back with a bloody nose. I made it over to the nurse's station, and they patched me up. I never made it to Vesper Hill that night, and I showed up at breakfast the next morning with a bandaged nose, and a long story of what happened. I still have a tiny scar from that incident, but even so, Camp Ohio remains one of my favorite places on earth.*
>
> Jim Cain
> Summer of 1975

For most of my adult life, I've been hanging out with the adventure crowd. Kayaking, rock climbing, rope courses, zip lines, white water rafting, hiking, winter camping, and more, and I've collected a few scars in my life as a result. This activity is much more about the life lessons and stories surrounding the injuries in our lives than the scars themselves. So celebrate these moments by sharing your stories with friends.

There is a scene in the movie Jaws, where the main characters are all in a boat, sharing stories of their lives and the scars they have collected along the way. I found the clip on MovieClips and YouTube with the search line "Jaws movie clip scars."

In the movie Galaxy Quest, Tim Allen's character activates the "Omega 13," a matter rearranger that allows for a 13-second leap to the past. Enough time to redeem a single mistake and similar to the "undo" button on your laptop computer. Question: if you could undo the event that caused your scar, would you?

49. MAGIC LAMP

*Legend states that if you find a magic lamp and rub it,
a Genie will appear and grant you three wishes.*

One of the things I love most about experiential education and adventure-based learning is the powerful use of metaphor. For this activity, you could just ask your audience what they would like to accomplish or experience today, but by using the magic lamp (a metaphor for making a wish), I've found audiences enjoy this opening activity much more than conversation alone. So I have begun packing a magic lamp in my training supplies now and use it with almost every group I facilitate.

When I lead this activity, I typically invite my audience to close their eyes and think of something that could happen today that would make their experience wonderful. The simple act of closing your eyes provides a quiet moment for participants to consider all the things that could contribute to their success today. Then, when everyone in the group has opened their eyes, I pass around the magic lamp and encourage everyone to share their thoughts. I mention that those who share their thoughts aloud are more likely to get their wish. This is a brilliant way for teachers, trainers, and facilitators to learn how to teach and reach their participants.

You can find plastic magic lamps, like those shown in the photographs, at a variety of places on the Internet, including Oriental Trading Company (www.orientaltrading.com) and Amazon.com.

50. FIVE PHOTOS

I've been using a clicker for the debriefing activity The Virtual Slideshow for decades now, and I wanted to find a way to use this tool for another part of my training programs, and here it is. Five Photos is an opportunity for your audience to share stories of their recent history using imaginary photographs.

Before smartphones and tablets and even computers were widely used, the slide projector was a familiar piece of technology used to project images (slides) for public presentations. A clicker was used to advance the next slide and show that image on a projection screen. In the more modern era, a clicker (or TV remote control) is used to change channels (and many other things) on TVs. For the sake of this activity, the clicker is used to "show" your imaginary image, so that you can narrate to your group what they are "seeing."

Present each of your groups with a clicker and invite them to share and describe five photos from their recent life. These could be real things that they actually photographed or just things that happened to them recently that they want to share with the group.

If imaginary photographs are not for you, you can use the digital photographs that most folks carry on their mobile phones. See activity number 25 in this book, Smartphone Activities.

You can find clickers for this activity at www.training-wheels.com and at many pet stores (they are also used for dog training).

Here are five recent photographs from my life and the stories that go along with them. First, I like to encourage unusual talents at camp. Spoon Hanging is a classic summer camp talent. Next is the playground I saw in Tasmania with the rather ironic "Do Not Climb" warning signs. I find such irony incredibly funny. Another funny sign comes from a rather remote area of Newfoundland. It was indeed a very rough road. Fourth on the list are the four Japanese guys I encountered while climbing Mount Rainier near Seattle, Washington. They had gone to Walmart and bought these Halloween costumes earlier that day and just had to try them out. Finally comes a moment of true wonder. Hundreds of people launching wish balloons in Chiang Mai, Thailand, during the Loi Krathong festival. The entire night sky was filled with these wish balloons roughly the size of a 55-gallon barrel.

51. MY PERSONAL PYRAMID

Here is a very simple way of inviting your audience to share their thoughts about character. Begin with a collection of cards on which words of character have been written. Then ask each member of your audience to create a six-card pyramid, based upon the following criteria.

The three cards at the bottom form the foundation. These cards express three traits that they currently possess. The two cards on the next level identify two traits with which they sometimes struggle or find difficult. The final card at the top of the pyramid is something to which they aspire.

After each participant has created their personal pyramid, invite them to share it with a partner or in a small group. On the opposite page, you'll find a group discussing the possibilities for their own personal pyramid.

Following are a few words that you might consider using on your cards:

Honesty	Balance	Grit
Responsibility	Diversity	Humor
Helpfulness	Integrity	Love
Citizenship	Courage	Humility
Determination	Respect	Creativity
Leadership	Patience	Teamwork
Empathy	Tenacity	Flexibility
Gratitude	Trust	Honor

For this activity, you can use the Teamwork & Teamplay Training Cards, available from www.healthylearning.com or www.training-wheels.com, or you can use index cards to make your own set of character-based words. You can also invite your participants to make their own cards for this activity.

52. METAPHORICALLY SPEAKING

To prepare for this activity, you'll need to fill a box with random objects—enough so that each person in your audience can have at least one object. You might include such things as: stuffed animals, toys, a wind-up alarm clock, a wooden spoon, keys, computer cables, a first aid kit, a cell phone, a candy bar, a combination lock, a hammer, batteries, plant food, string, tools, rubber bands, and many of the other things you probably already have in your junk drawer at home.

Invite each person in your audience to take one of these items from the box. Then propose a topic for the group to consider, such as teamwork. Next, provide an example for the group using one of the objects.

Teamwork is like a piece of rope. The individual filaments cannot lift much weight by themselves, but when they join together, they can do so much more!

Then invite everyone in your audience to share as they metaphorically connect their object to the topic at hand. Don't be surprised if occasionally some of the metaphorical connections are indeed profound.

Duct tape is like The Force. It has a light side and a dark side, and it holds the universe together.

One of my favorite places on earth is the Buckeye Leadership Workshop (BLW) held annually in March in central Ohio, and one of my favorite people there is Christy Leeds, a member of the BLW planning committee. Christy once shared this metaphorical activity at the annual workshop. She told me she had witnessed this activity at a Cooperative Extension event at The Ohio State University, specifically related to the topic of program evaluation, but you can use it to frame any topic (such as leadership, teamwork, solving problems, relationships, building community, etc.).

53. BEST / WORST / FIRST

My favorite way to introduce this activity is to present one-third of the audience with an index card on which has been written the following information:

> **Best / Worst / First**
>
> Collect two other people and discuss the following information:
>
> What was your *best* meal ever?
>
> What was your *worst* summer job?
>
> Tell me about your *first* day of work.
>
> What is the *best* book you have ever read?
>
> What was the *worst* movie that you still watched from beginning to end?
>
> What would be your ideal *first* date?

This simple technique will place one-third of your audience in a leadership role. If time allows, you can include additional questions on the backside of each card, such as:

Where was the *best* hotel you have ever visited?

What was the *worst* weather you have ever experienced?

What was the *first* thing you ever purchased using a credit card?

What day of your life was the *best* ever?

What food was the *worst* you have ever eaten?

What was the *first* time you traveled outside your country?

At a recent leadership conference in Virginia, the keynote speaker suggested that there are three things that each one of us uniquely owns: our name, our reputation, and our stories. Best / Worst / First is an opportunity for people to share their personal stories.

Acronyms & Abbreviations

None of us is as smart as all of us!

See if your group can discover the true meanings of the following acronyms.

1. NASA
2. SCUBA
3. NASCAR
4. LASER
5. VOIP
6. ROI
7. TNT
8. PDF
9. Wi-Fi
10. SASE
11. DVD
12. RSVP
13. NATO
14. UNICEF
15. POTUS
16. TASER
17. MODEM
18. RADAR
19. ISBN
20. OSHA

54. ACRONYMS & ABBREVIATIONS

Feel free to make copies of the information shown on the opposite page. You will need one copy of this page for each group of three people. Sharing resources is part of working together as a team. Allow each group of three to work on this challenge for about five minutes, and then encourage each small group to "double their brainpower" by combining with another nearby group (to form a group of six).

A teachable moment in this activity is realizing that none of us is as smart as all of us. If we work together, we can accomplish much more than any single individual can.

One of the variations I like for this activity helps to reduce the competition that sometimes occurs when teams are working on a challenge with other teams nearby. After doubling the brainpower of each group of three, creating a group of six, I invite one person from each group of six to come together as ambassadors for their group. When the ambassadors gather together, they can discuss the acronyms they have solved and look for help in the ones they still need to decode. After a minute or two, I send the ambassadors back to their groups and allow another minute or two to finish the activity, before sharing the answers provided.

Here are the solutions to the acronyms and abbreviations of the opposite page.

1. National Aeronautics and Space Administration
2. Self-Contained Underwater Breathing Apparatus (best acronym ever!)
3. North American Stock Car Auto Racing
4. Light Amplification by Simulated Emission of Radiation
5. Voice Over Internet Protocol
6. Return on Investment
7. Trinitrotoluene
8. Portable Document Format
9. Wireless Fidelity
10. Self-Addressed Stamped Envelope
11. Digital Versatile (Video) Disc
12. Respondez S'il Vous Plait
13. North Atlantic Treaty Organization
14. United Nations International Children's Emergency Fund
15. President of the United States
16. Thomas A. Swift Electronic Rifle
17. Modulator - Demodulator
18. Radio Detection and Ranging
19. International Standard Book Number
20. Occupational Safety and Healthy Administration

55. DRAW ME YOUR STORY

A picture is worth a thousand words.

Here is a get-acquainted activity invites partners to learn about each other by drawing pictures rather than speaking. First, present each group of two people with one large piece of paper and one marker or crayon. Next, ask them to take turns drawing a picture of each of the following items:

The house where you grew up	Your vehicle
Something you wish for	Your favorite hobby
A map of where you now live	A sport you enjoy
Your family	Your favorite food

After completing the drawing part of this activity, you can invite partners to ask each other questions about their drawings and share insights.

I first experienced this activity at an Outward Bound International Symposium in Ontario, Canada. Andy Martin, author of Outdoor and Experiential Learning (ISBN 978-0-5660-8628-X), shared this activity from his collection of holistic and drama-based learning, many of which are part of the Inner Touch program of Outward Bound Czech Republic.

If you enjoy this activity, you might also enjoy reading the book, *Show Me a Story: 40 Craft Projects and Activities to Spark Children's Storytelling* by Emily Neuburger (ISBN 978-1-6034-2988-7).

Opening Thoughts & Closing Questions

A Final Reviewing Activity From Teamwork & Teamplay

What do you want to see happen as we continue to build relationships with each other in the workplace? How can we continue to do this, and why should we?

What are some current barriers to this happening?

What do you want to tell your leaders about today?

Did anyone in your group do a particularly great job today? Tell us about them.

Top Insights (three things you'll take away from this experience):

1.

2.

3.

56. END-OF-THE-DAY QUESTIONS

As a facilitator, I am sometimes challenged to find the perfect closing activity or final debriefing technique for any particular group. Or at least I was until I discovered this foolproof debriefing technique. Instead of randomly choosing one of my favorite closing activities or preparing general reviewing questions in advance, I simply ask a group at the start of the program what questions they would like to ask themselves at the end of the day.

Sometimes I pass out index cards and pencils to every participant and ask them to write down one or two questions for their own private review. Other times, I stand at the front of the group with a flipchart and record three or four questions (like those shown on the opposite page). I keep this list visible throughout the day, so that participants are reminded that we will discuss these questions at the end of the day.

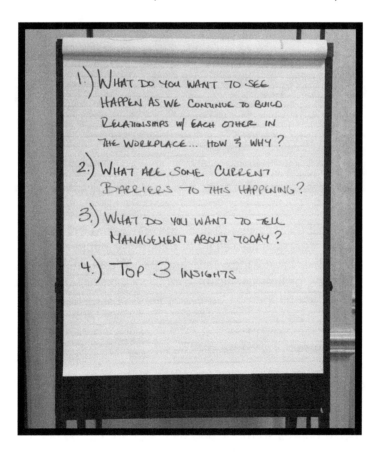

You are welcome to make copies of the Opening Thoughts & Closing Questions on the opposite page for your next group. For many corporate groups, I share the information collected on these documents with the group managers or leaders at the end of the program. A valuable feedback technique, indeed.

57. FIVE EVENTS THAT SHAPED MY LIFE

Many icebreakers and get-acquainted activities can be sedentary. Personally, I like a little movement so for this activity, let's use the "walking and talking" technique. Begin by inviting everyone to find a partner and take a stroll with them around the room. As they walk, instruct everyone to share five significant events that have shaped their lives. Continue walking and talking until both partners have shared five events.

A second version of this activity requires less space and movement, but a bit more artistic content. This version works well if your audience happens to be seated. Simply provide everyone with a large index card and pencil/pen/marker/crayon, and invite them to draw sketches of five significant events in their life and share these with a nearby partner, or if they happen to have a smartphone or tablet, draw an electronic sketch instead.

As I was writing this activity, I reflected on five significant events in my own life. Here they are, in no particular order. I joined 4-H as a kid, and because of this I had exposure to many leadership opportunities (and I still help with 4-H programs whenever I can). I play guitar and call square dances so music and dancing have always been a part of my life. I wrote my doctoral dissertation and my first book (Teamwork & Teamplay) the same year, and both have opened many doors for me. My work with the American Camping Association and the International Camping Fellowship has taken me around the world several times. And, I have creative, artistic friends that bring great joy to my life.

58. BROKEN TOKEN

*Token: n. A visible or tangible representation
(a symbol) of a fact or feeling.*

A Broken Token is an object that has been cut into two (or more) pieces. When all the pieces are reunited, the token becomes whole again.

I like to use the Broken Token activity as a creatively random way to form groups at the start of a program. With a little preparation, you can create groups from 2 to 10 people with ease. First, you'll need to decide what group size you would ideally like to create. Next, you'll need to collect sufficient "stuff" so that every person in the group received one of these items. The stuff can be a wide variety of objects that go together, such as:

*comic strips, jigsaw puzzle pieces, wood blocks cut into unique
shapes, playing cards that have been uniquely cut in half, paint
color sample cards, nuts and bolts, photographs, index cards
with half a quote or half a word*

As an example, let's use a variety of sizes of nuts and bolts (see photo below). Randomly place these into a large bowl and invite everyone in your audience to take one and then find the other people in their group. For groups of four you will need one bolt and three nuts that fit this bolt.

As a second example, consider the three-dimensional jigsaw puzzle made from the wood block shown here. This particular block has a total of 12 pieces and requires a bit more puzzle and problem solving skill to find the other members of your group. You can make these blocks on a bandsaw using different varieties of wood and different sizes of blocks. Some woods even have a distinctive smell.

See activity number 101 in this book for more ideas how to use nuts and bolts for teambuilding challenges.

59. EMOTIONAL WEATHER REPORT

This opening activity is a metaphorical technique for describing everyone's current status in meteorological terms. Perhaps you find yourself sunny and bright this morning or a bit foggy or partly cloudy. Verbal input is sufficient for this activity, but if you want to enhance the experience, include photographs, drawings, illustrations, or graphics of various weather conditions.

You can find some pretty amazing weather photographs and graphics on the Internet. Try searching "amazing weather photography" and other weather-related terms. You can also create your own deck of Emotional Weather Report cards for conditions ranging from sunny and warm to dark and stormy, and everything in between. Choose weather conditions that are typical for your part of the world.

If weather patterns are not a reasonable metaphor for your group, consider using traffic signs instead. There are tons of actual traffic signs available on the Internet, as well as quite a few funny ones as well. If you enjoy this kind of humor, see the collection of absurd and amusing signs from around the world in the book *Signspotting* 2 (ISBN 978-1-7417-9182-2) compiled by Doug Lansky. You can use any of these traffic signs as metaphors for the journey your group plans to take today.

60. BACKSIDE WRITING

Backside Writing (or Butt Writing, as some refer to it) is simply that. Participants turn their backs to the audience and introduce themselves by writing their first name using their bottom as the imaginary writing tool. The audience then tries to guess the name of the writer. Some audience members have been heard to say, "We didn't quite get that. Could you do it again?" for particularly challenging displays of backside legibility. A very funny way to introduce yourself, indeed.

If spelling your name with your backside isn't the ideal activity for your next group, you can try using your head (Melon Spellin') instead.

Disclaimer: I have tried very hard in this book to select icebreakers and other activities that I believe are the very best. In most cases, I have avoided those activities that I consider foolish, but with this particular activity, well, I just couldn't resist!

I first witnessed this activity at a police conference in Auckland, New Zealand. The Blue Light organization encourages police in New Zealand, Australia, and the UK to interact in positive ways with youth (community dances, school projects, camps, fun days). During the Blue Light International Conference, the event moderator invited a few members of the audience to join him on stage and introduce themselves to the entire audience of 300+ people by writing their name with their bottom. This included dotting the i and crossing the t when necessary. So I figured if 300-plus highly trained, professionally dignified police personnel can do this activity, then so can we!

100 Activities That Build Unity, Community & Connection • Jim Cain

61. CAPTAIN NEMO

It turns out that Captain Nemo, Jules Verne's fictional antihero from the novel *20,000 Leagues Under the Sea* likes to go to parties in disguise, and he stays only until he is discovered. In the game that follows, your audience will try to find Captain Nemo.

Invite your group of 20 to 30 people to close their eyes. Then walk around the group and designate one person to be Captain Nemo by tapping them on the shoulder. When your audience opens their eyes, tell them they are to shake hands with everyone they meet, asking, "Are you Nemo?"

The first five times Captain Nemo shakes hands, his reply to "Are you Nemo?" is no! But on the sixth handshake, he says (loudly) "Yes!" When this happens, Nemo's sixth handshake partner quickly lines up behind Nemo, placing both hands on Nemo's shoulders. When the audience sees this happen, they quickly get in line behind Nemo and his partner, trying not to be the last person in line.

This game is perhaps the fastest (and most fun) way to organize any group into a line. So the next time you need your group in a line, try searching for Captain Nemo, and your group will actually enjoy getting into line. This activity also requires plenty of open space. If you happen to have more than 30 people, consider splitting into two groups to play this rambunctious game.

Mark Collard is a brilliant trainer and player of games from Australia. Mark shared this game with me and mentioned that it is always one of the most popular games on his website (www.playmeo.com or www.markcollard.com). You can find more of Mark's wonderful games in his books *No Props* (ISBN 0-934387-05-02) and *Count Me In* (ISBN 978-0-934387-30-9).

62. THE BOX

The Box is an artistic way to represent your inner and outer self. On the outside of a plain cardboard box (available at many packaging stores, stationery stores, and stores that carry gift boxes), participants write the gifts they share with society, using words, images, stickers, and other artistic content. This can include skills, abilities, knowledge, and other external talents that are typically public knowledge or often shared freely within groups.

On the inside of the box, participants place internal things that typically only they know about themselves. This can include skills and talents, but also a variety of other things known only to the box's owner.

When everyone has created their box, invite individual participants to share the external (outside) attributes. As trust is built within the group, you can invite participants to begin sharing some of the internal (inside) attributes with the other members of the group.

If you don't happen to have suitable cardboard boxes for this activity, you can improvise with ordinary brown paper lunch bags or envelopes—drawing on the outside the many things that are public and on the inside those things that are personal or private.

More than a decade ago, Barbara Decker of the Voyages Summer Institute in St. Louis shared this marvelous activity with me. With her permission, I am glad to share these variations of her contribution with the world.

63. BALLOON BOP FOR THREE

This gentle physical warm-up activity is one of my favorite ways to get a group moving in the morning. Provide each group of three people with an inflated balloon. Ask them to hold hands throughout the activity and keep their balloon in the air, at first using only their hands. Continue this activity, but occasionally change the body part contacting the balloon, in the following order:

    Hands Only
    Elbows Only
    Elbows and Heads
    Knees Only
    Knees and Feet
    And finally, using only your breath!

This simple activity will not only provide a physical warm-up for your group, it also encourages communication, teamwork, quick thinking, and problem solving.

If your group is talented at this activity, you might try one with slightly more challenge, such as the Peteca activity in this book.

64. CHOO-CHOO, WHO ARE YOU?

Here is a convenient activity for organizing one large group into several equal-sized smaller groups. It is also a TPR (Total Physical Response) technique for quickly learning and remembering the names of the people in your group.

Begin with your entire audience in one large circle. Next, identify a select number of "Engineers" to step into the circle. Choose the same number of Engineers as the number of groups you wish to create.

Each Engineer approaches a member of the large circle and holding both hands says, "Choo-choo, who are you?" The new member of the forming train says their name, "Meghan." Then Meghan and the Engineer repeat her name five times, "Meghan, Meghan, Meghan-Meghan-Meghan." At this point, the Engineer turns around (facing the center of the large circle), Meghan places her hands on the Jim Engineer's shoulders, and this pair moves off in search of another person to join their train.

Each time a "train" reaches a person in the large circle, they join hands, exchange names, and repeat the process until everyone in the large circle has joined a train.

This activity is one of the oldest name games I know. If you'd like to find more games from the past, my favorite place to look is www.archive.org. On this website, you can search for books, videos, and other documentation both recent and ancient. I found many game books over 100 years old here, in easy-to-download digital formats that I can read on my smartphone, tablet, or computer for free!

If you want to know more about Total Physical Response, a language teaching method based on the coordination of language and physical movement, visit: www.trp-world.com.

65. STORY TAGS

If you have ever attended a conference or meeting, you have no doubt seen participants wearing some version of the classic "Hello, my name is _____" nametag. This activity goes well beyond the ordinary nametag by inviting participants to share more information about themselves than just their name. Space is provided on each Story Tag for not only the name of the individual, but also elements of "their story," such as their family, hobbies, education, career, college major, sports, music, recreational activities, animals, favorite foods, etc.

The Story Tag becomes an invitation each time you encounter new people to share the various elements with others and listen as they share with you.

Story Tags can be hand drawn with bright colorful markers and stickers, ribbons, and other colorful additions can also be attached.

In my book Rope Games, I mentioned that one of the most significant rope activities I discovered on the Internet was the Story Rope, where participants used a variety of objects to construct a rope and then use that rope to tell the story of their life. A very creative story telling technique, indeed. For more information about Story Ropes, visit: www.margemalwitz.blogspot.com.

Also, Debi Hitter of Castleton, New York, hand-carves hardwood walking sticks as Life History Sticks, carefully (and colorfully) carving various moments of people's lives into a useful and beautiful walking stick. For more information, contact Debi at: www.mssticks.com.

66. HALL OF FAME STATUES

*You can learn more about a person in an hour
of play than in a year of conversation.*

I like to have activities ready the minute my first participant walks through the door. It rewards the people who arrive early and immediately involves everyone in the room. I also like to assess my group by watching how they work and play together in the very first activity. The Hall of Fame Statue project is my favorite way to begin a program, especially when I have limited knowledge of the group in advance.

Organize your audience into smaller groups of six people, and supply each group with some type of construction kit. Inform each group that a new sport Hall of Fame (basketball, baseball, hockey, soccer) is being built, but lacks a statue for the main lobby. Then challenge each group to create a statue using the construction materials supplied. I like to keep the time limit on this activity short (about five minutes) to keep the activity and energy level high.

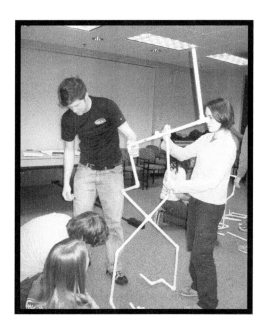

You can use a variety of building blocks, construction kits (such as TinkerToys, Lincoln Logs, or LEGO blocks) for this activity. The PVC tubes and connectors shown in the photos here are Teamplay Tubes, designed by Jim Cain and available from: www.training-wheels.com.

Not far from where I live, a major toy company still has a room in their corporate offices with one-way glass mirrors, where they can observe as children interact with their toys. You can learn quite a bit about your audience by watching how they play together during this statue building activity.

CHAPTER 3

Activities That Create Teachable Moments

This chapter contains active ways to create teachable moments as you build unity, community, and connection with your group. These activities will help you explore such topics as: trust building, teamwork, communication, creative problem solving, adapting to change, goal setting, character building, and more.

No.	Activity Name	Teachable Moment	Ideal Group Size
67	Giant Jigsaw Puzzle	Communication, Teamwork	6 to 8 People per Puzzle
68	Arrowheads	Problem Solving	3 to 6 People per Puzzle
69	Sunny Side Up	Teamwork, Problem Solving	6 to 8 People per Tarp
70	Bandana Island	Teambuilding in Tight Spaces	4 People per Bandana
71	Not Knots / The Missing Link	Decision Making	10 or More People
72	Part of the Rainbow	A Visual Challenge	6 or More People
73	Three Chairs	Win/Win Situations	15 or More People
74	Quotes in Order	A Linguistic Challenge	Any
75	Match Cards	Building Character	Multiple Groups of 6+
76	Wobble	Fun and Games	6 People per Kit
77	Magic Carpet	Problem Solving, Teamwork	10 People per Carpet
78	A Perfect Match	Communication	12 People per Group
79	Blind Trust Drive	Trust Building	Partners
80	Petecas	Active Teamwork	10 People per Peteca
81	The Bobsled Team	Active Teamwork	Multiple Teams of 4
82	Bull Ring Community	Teamwork	3 Teams of 12 People
83	Word Circles	A Linguistic Challenge	Any
84	Spiral Walk	Communication, Trust	Partners

For this activity, you can make your own giant jigsaw puzzle from wood or cardboard or purchase a Blindfolded Giant Jigsaw Puzzle and colorful Lycra blindfolds from Training Wheels, Inc. at: www.training-wheels.com.

You will find this activity and 99 more in the book *Teambuilding Puzzles* (ISBN 978-0-7575-7040-7) by Mike Anderson, Jim Cain, Chris Cavert, and Tom Heck, available from www.kendallhunt.com and www.healthylearning.com. You can also find a few more jigsaw puzzle variations in this book to challenge your audiences.

67. GIANT JIGSAW PUZZLE

This teambuilding challenge invites a small group to assemble a jigsaw puzzle. Sounds easy, right? Okay, then, let's add a higher level of challenge. Let's complete this activity blindfolded.

Begin this activity with a group of 6 to 10 people sitting in a small circle on the floor. If you happen to have more than 10 people, invite the extras to be observers in this activity. Next, provide blindfolds to the group, or ask those seated to close their eyes. Then inform the group that you have some "stuff" and you would like them to put it together. All the necessary pieces are within arm's reach of your present position, so there is no need to move around, and you can ask three questions during the completion of this task. Then place most of the jigsaw pieces in the center of the circle. Quietly place three pieces outside the circle and hold one piece just above the head of one of the participants. In this manner, all pieces are within arm's reach but obviously some outside-the-box thinking needs to occur to find them all. Once all pieces are in place, tell your group to begin.

As a variation, you can paint inspirational words or pictures on the surface of the puzzle so that when it is completed the group will be able to view the final image.

When construction of the puzzle is complete, ask participants to remove their blindfolds. Then ask the observers to be the first to share their observations with the group. Then allow the participants to share their impressions. Who displayed leadership during the activity? Who created a workable plan? Who identified that the object was a puzzle? Who managed to place together the first two pieces?

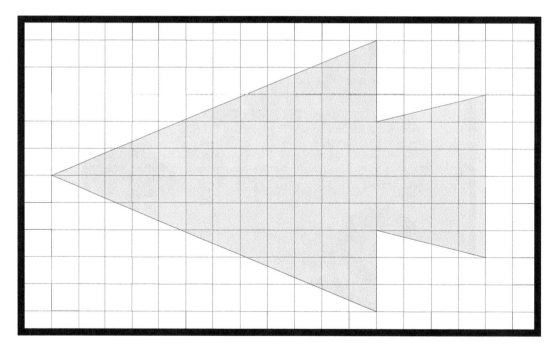

You can create your own arrowhead puzzle using the template above. Photocopy this template and enlarge it to the size you desire, and then transfer the pattern to a piece of wood or cardboard. One arrowhead is whole, the other three are cut into two pieces as shown in the photos above.

68. ARROWHEADS

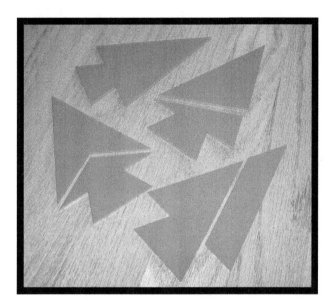

Here is a challenging puzzle for exploring the concepts of limited resources. If your team needs to successfully complete a task when there seems to be insufficient resources to do so, then this is the perfect team challenge for you. You can make your own Arrowhead puzzle from the template provided on the opposite page.

Using the seven puzzle pieces shown here, simultaneously assemble five arrowheads. One arrowhead is already complete, and provides a size template for the remaining arrowheads. Each of the four remaining arrowheads will be the same size and shape as this one. When you are finished, you will be able to see all five arrowheads at the same time.

Most groups struggle to create four different arrowheads and then typically comment to the facilitator that, "There aren't enough pieces to make a fifth arrowhead." To which you can reply, "You have sufficient resources to complete the task." Of course, this requires some out-of-the-box thinking. You can further assist your team with clues such as, "It is important to get your arrowheads pointed in the same direction," or "In our group, we like to march in a two-by-two formation."

The solution to this puzzle comes from using each available resource to create more than just one arrowhead. In this case, the four primary arrowheads can be assembled in a two-by-two pattern to frame a fifth arrowhead in the center. The contribution of each individual arrowhead is *more* than just one! This is a synergistic relationship.

At this point. you can debrief this activity or further explore synergy by asking the group, "If we combine four of these puzzles, how many arrowheads can we produce?" The answer: an amazing 25! As shown in a photo on the opposite page.

Underwater Arrowheads

This variation of the Arrowhead activity is a bit more challenging. While this activity actually takes place on dry land, it does require some underwater skills. Begin with the entire team standing around the perimeter of a long rope, 100 feet (30 meters) in length. In the center of the rope circle, seven large Arrowhead pieces are placed randomly on a table. The task for the group is to correctly assemble these seven pieces to make five Arrowheads (just as in the previous version of the activity). The challenge is that team members can only enter the circle one person at a time and they must hold their breath for the duration of the time they are inside the circle. The circle is essentially an imaginary swimming pool and the Arrowhead pieces are "underwater." Since participants cannot hear underwater, communication can only occur on dry land (outside the perimeter of the circle). By requiring participants to only stay inside the circle for as long as they can hold their breath, facilitators encourage all group members to become involved in the solution process, not just a select few.

Creating Teachable Moments With Puzzles

The teachable moment in this activity comes from realizing that, even when there appears to be insufficient resources, if you use the resources you have creatively, you can often do more with less. Let's take this concept a step further, and graphically illustrate exactly what collaboration and synergy can mean to your organization. Imagine that you have one employee creating the training manuals for your organization. With the recent hiring of more employees, you are going to need more manuals very soon, so you hire nine additional employees to perform this task. You're good at math, so you calculate that if one employee can produce 10 training manuals in a week, then 10 employees should be able to produce 100 training manuals in that same week. While the mathematics in this example is simple, the organizational culture is not. For some organizations a tenfold increase in manpower will yield a tenfold increase in output. For synergistic organizations that are efficient, a tenfold increase in manpower can yield greater than a tenfold increase in output. Unfortunately, this same concept works in reverse. For organizations that are struggling, a tenfold increase in manpower not only does not produce a tenfold increase in output, but the overall efficiency of the entire organization goes down with change.

Graphically, this information looks like the illustration. The real goal then is to create the kind of environment where additional staff members not only cover their share of the work, but enhance the output of others in the organization. As a reviewing tool for the Arrowhead Puzzle, make a list with your staff about which factors contribute to a positive culture and environment and which ones create a negative return on investment. This is the ideal place to discuss attitude, behavior, individual contributions, and team performance. By identifying those factors that not only contribute to a positive atmosphere, but also those that diminish it, your team can create a strategy for keeping their work environment positive and rewarding. Keep this list in a public place in your organization. And when someone demonstrates a behavior not in keeping with the group's ideals, reinforce the positive cultural values your group helped create.

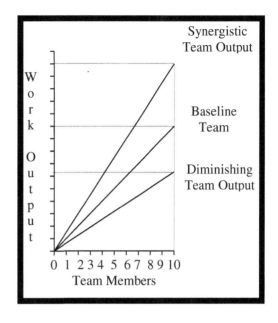

The Arrowhead Puzzle is a great activity to help your team understand the value of synergy. Synergy can be described metaphorically as: 1 + 1 = 3. Synergy exists when the output of a team is greater than the output of each individual combined. The illustration above demonstrates this point. If one team member can produce one unit of output and we hire nine additional team members, we expect to be able to produce a total output of 10 units. If our team members work synergistically, they can actually produce more than 10 units of output. Conversely, if our team members do not work synergistically or even worse, reduce each other's effectiveness, less than 10 units of output will be produced. From this simple analysis, you can see that teams operating synergistically have a substantial advantage over teams that do not.

You will find this activity and 50 more in the book *Essential Staff Training Activity* (ISBN 978-0-7575-6167-2) by Jim Cain, Clare Marie Hannon, and David Knobbe. You can find more puzzles that create teachable moments in the book *Teambuilding Puzzles* (ISBN 978-0-7575-7040-7) by Mike Anderson, Jim Cain, Chris Cavert, and Tom Heck. And you can find out more information about teachable moments in the book *A Teachable Moment* (ISBN 978-0-7575-1782-2) by Jim Cain, Michelle Cummings, and Jennifer Stanchfield. All of these books are available from www.kendallhunt.com and www.healthylearning.com.

69. SUNNY SIDE UP

This teambuilding challenge is easy to explain, but not necessarily easy to complete. Supply a group of 10 people with a small tarp, and invite them to hold on around the perimeter. Then place a tennis ball in the center of the tarp. Inform the group that their task is to use the tarp to toss the ball into the air, flip over the tarp, and catch the ball on the way back down.

If necessary, you can substitute a plastic shower curtain, tablecloth, or blanket for the tarp, and a stuffed animal or soft toy for the tennis ball.

To encourage your group to plan their work before working their plan, I like to explain the task, but then withhold the ball until they can demonstrate their proposed technique. When they feel that they have a plan with at least a 50/50 chance of success, I give them the ball.

If your group is successful with a single tennis ball and you want to give them a higher a level of challenge, try this activity with two tennis balls. You can also challenge your group to catch a single ball twice in a row or see if they can toss the ball high enough to flip the tarp over twice and still catch the ball.

One element of a truly effective teambuilding activity is the feeling of accomplishment that accompanies the successful completion of the task. While it is possible to roll the ball onto the opposite side by carefully folding the tarp, this particular solution does not create much enthusiasm. In contrast, groups that successfully toss the ball, flip the tarp, and catch the ball typically scream with excitement and celebrate their success. For me, it is all about the energy created that makes this one of my favorite teambuilding activities.

I did not actually "invent" this activity, I just observed a group playing with a tarp and ball and imagined it. During a *Teamwork & Teamplay* workshop with social workers in Missouri, I had equipped several groups with tarps and tennis balls. Just as I did this, the caterer showed up. As I was coordinating our lunch plans, I watched as several groups began using their tarps to toss multiple tennis balls into the air. They were so happy, and their energy was amazing. Rather than stopping their spontaneous play, I simply thought of a way to use that energy for something related to teambuilding. And that was how Sunny Side Up was invented and became one of my favorite team challenges.

Recently, I was invited to assist a summer camp program in Guilin, China. The campers at this particular camp were quite young. I realized that a tennis ball would be too much of a challenge for this age group, so I replaced it with a balloon. The slow movement of the balloon gave my campers much more time to flip the tarp. Their enthusiasm was amazing the first time they caught the balloon.

70. BANDANA ISLAND

One of the attributes of a successful team challenge activity is that it is easy to explain but challenging to complete. Bandana Island is exactly that type of activity.

Begin by placing a standard bandana flat on the floor and then place four coins randomly on top of the bandana. Next, invite four people to stand completely on the bandana so that no part of their shoes touches the floor. Then challenge each person to reach down and pick up one coin without any of the four people touching the floor with any part of their body throughout the activity.

Cooperation, communication, problem solving, and teamwork are necessary skills in this activity. Many teams discover that this activity is made substantially easier when team members help each other by spotting, holding each other up, and moving out of the way when necessary.

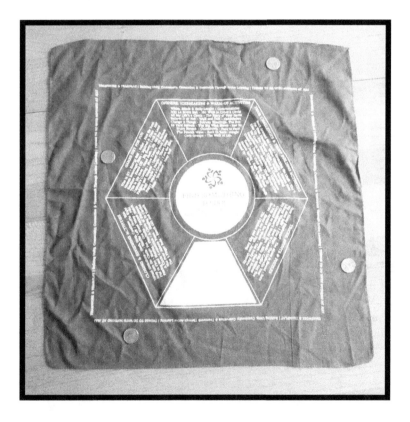

The *Teamwork & Teamplay* bandanas shown here contain a list of all the no-prop activities found in the book *Find Something To Do* by Jim Cain, available from www.training-wheels.com and www.healthylearning.com. FSTD bandanas are available from www.teamworkandteamplay.com.

71. NOT KNOTS / THE MISSING LINK

Here are two consensus-building activities that produce great results with minimal props.

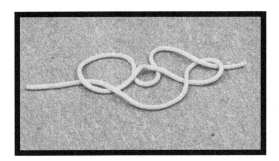
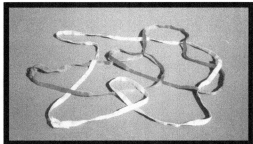

Not Knots

This activity requires only a short piece of rope (about 8 feet). The facilitator prepares a rope tangle in advance (see photo), and group members try to decide what will happen when the ends of the rope are pulled part. Those that believe a knot will form stand on the left side; those that believe no knot will form stand on the right. In most cases, there will be participants on both sides. The real challenge is to create consensus between these two groups. Invite one person from each side to form a partnership and collectively decide which side to go to together. Then pull the ends of the rope to display the result.

The Missing Link

This activity uses two knotted Raccoon Circles of different colors. The facilitator again prepares the tangle in advance. This time, individuals must decide whether the two Raccoon Circles are connected (linked) or disconnected (unlinked) when they are pulled apart. Invite partnerships between both sides and encourage the entire group to achieve consensus. Then attempt to separate the two rope circles and discover whether they are linked or unlinked.

If you enjoy these simple teambuilding challenges with ropes, you might enjoy an entire book filled with similar activities. *Rope Games* by Jim Cain is available from Healthy Learning (www.healthy-learning.com) and Training Wheels, Inc. (www.training-wheels.com). There is also the *Rope Games* Kit available from Training Wheels, Inc.

72. PART OF THE RAINBOW

Do you see what I see?

To prepare for this activity, you will need to collect a dozen or more of the paint color samples available at most paint or hardware stores. Fasten these samples to a bulletin board or wall at eye level. We will call these samples "the collection." Then take a duplicate of just one of these color samples and fasten it to a different bulletin board or wall that is not in direct line of sight with the collection. We will call this single sample "the target."

Next, invite one member of the group at a time to travel to the target and return to the collection. When everyone has had the opportunity to view the target sample, then invite them to make their best guess which of the collection samples most closely represents the target sample.

The first time I present this activity to a group, I like to set them up for success by making the target a familiar primary color (red, blue, or yellow), and the collection of samples a full rainbow of possibilities. Most folks are unlikely to mistake blue for green, but you never know.

For the second round, I increase the challenge by making the target a subtle shade of blue or green and all of the collection samples variations of this same color. A much more difficult challenge, indeed.

Note: some group members may try to use more than just their eyesight and memory to record the target color by comparing the target to a piece of clothing they are wearing or taking a smartphone photograph are both creative possibilities.

After groups have reached consensus or at least determined their best guess, remove the target sample and bring it back to the collection for an accurate determination of the matching color sample.

This is the first time I've included this activity in one of my teambuilding publications. It explores the possibility that two or more people can look at the same things and yet see something different. This can lead to some very interesting debriefing content as your group explores such things as a common vision and what consensus or agreement will look like for this group.

73. THREE CHAIRS

This activity presents an interesting debrief since most groups tend to compete for resources in this activity, rather than searching for a win-win solution. Begin the activity by dividing your group into three equal parts. Each group is then provided with one of the following commands:

> Place all the chairs in the room in a circle.
>
> Turn all the chairs in the room on their side.
>
> Move all the chairs to one corner of the room.

After each group has been given their command, encourage them to quickly perform the task they are assigned. Chaos typically happens as the three teams try to gather as many resources (chairs) as they can to complete their task. This chaos leads to a perfect opportunity to debrief the activity with a discussion about achieving win-win solutions when practical, which in this case might involve placing all the chairs on their side, in a circle, in one corner of the room.

This activity works best if you happen to have these three essential elements: 20 to 30 chairs, a room with four corners, and 20 to 30 competitive people.

I discovered this activity in Europe, where it is very familiar with trainers and facilitators there. You can find this activity and 50 other activities in *The Teamwork & Teamplay International Edition* by Jim Cain (ISBN 978-0-9882046-3-8) available from www.healthylearning.com and www.training-wheels.com. This book includes 51 team activities and translations in 16 languages, including: Chinese, Japanese, Russian, Turkish, Greek, Hebrew, Danish, Thai, Mongolian, Spanish, French, German, Dutch, Italian, Portuguese, and English.

74. QUOTES IN ORDER

"Problems worthy of attack, prove their worth by fighting back."

—Piet Hein

The goal of this linguistic challenge is for a team to place various word cards in the proper sequence to replicate a popular quotation. On the opposite page, you'll find a Piet Hein quotation mixed in the first photograph and correctly sequenced in the second one.

Each school year, many teachers place inspirational posters in their classrooms, but after a week or two, most students barely look at them. Quotes in Order engages students by challenging them to make sense of the quotation as they struggle to properly sequence what at first appears as a random jumble of words. The greater the engagement during the learning process, the greater the retention of the information itself.

You can find hundreds of quotations at websites such as: www.quotationspage.com. These sites allow you to search using keywords like: teamwork, leadership, communication, trust, etc. Then create your own Quotes in Order activity props by transferring these quotes to index cards, with one or two words per card.

"The two most important days in your life are the day you were born, and the day you find out why."

—Mark Twain

"The illiterate of the 21st century will not be those who cannot read and write, but those who cannot learn, unlearn, and relearn."

—Alvin Toffler

"Never doubt that a small group of thoughtful, committed citizens can change the world; indeed it's the only thing that ever has."

—Margaret Mead

If you enjoy teambuilding with index cards, keep an eye on the *Teamwork & Teamplay* website (www.teamworkandteamplay.com) for news of Jim Cain's next book, *Teambuilding With Index Cards*, featuring 100 activities for teachers, trainers, facilitators, and group leaders of all kinds that turn ordinary index and playing cards into extraordinary teaching tools.

75. MATCH CARDS

Match Cards are a variation of the memory game. Twelve different word pairs are written on 24 index cards, and these cards are randomly placed face down on a table. You will need one collection of these cards for each group you have present. At the beginning of the activity, one team member approaches their table and turns over any two cards, revealing the words. If the words match, the cards are placed in their original position face up. If the words do not match, the cards are turned face down in their original position. Then the second person repeats this pattern. The first team to turn over all 24 cards is the winner. But the real value of this game is that the same cards used as props during the game become the debriefing tool at the completion of the game.

In the first stage of the debriefing, ask each person to select one card that contains a word or phrase they believe is important. Then invite each person to explain why that word or phrase is important to them. In the second stage, ask each group to decide which five words of the 12 present are the five most important words to them. Turn some cards face down but leave five cards face up, containing the five words or phrases selected by the entire group. And finally, in stage three, ask the group which word on these five cards they could absolutely not live without.

While the actual words and phrases presented on the cards are important, it is the discussion that happens within the group that is often the most valuable component of this activity.

Here are examples of some words you might include in your cards:

Teamwork – Communication – Respect – Diversity – Trust – Integrity

Leadership – Responsibility – Honesty – Character – Grit – Cooperation

---

A few years ago, I presented a series of teambuilding workshops for a major corporation. In one department of about 30 people, the culture had eroded to the point where the daily stress was overwhelming. After using a variety of team and community building activities, I happened to present Match Cards, using a collection of 24 index cards on which I had written words of character, such as: respect, responsibility, trust, honesty, integrity, communication, leadership, and teamwork. While the activity itself had the desired effect, it was the debriefing after the activity that truly transformed the group. No doubt this was one of the most powerful teambuilding experiences I have ever witnessed.

The *Teamwork & Teamplay Training Cards* have 26 different word pairs that you can use for this activity (and 16 more activities, too!). You can purchase these cards from Healthy Learning (www.healthylearning.com) and Training Wheels, Inc. (www.training-wheels.com).

76. WOBBLE

Wobble is a simple game (similar to lawn bowling) that you can make yourself from PVC tubing and other easy-to-find supplies. The game consists of a small white PVC tube target (known as the jack) and six larger PVC tubes (wobbles) that have been specifically cut to be unbalanced (they wobble when rolled) and painted six different colors. The goal of the game is to capture the jack with your wobble, with collecting (and occasionally losing) points along the way. Scores are kept with a wooden clothespin the same color as your wobble on a ruler. First person to score 12 points wins.

Rules of Play

Toss the jack 20 feet (6 meters) away.
Players take turns rolling (tossing, throwing) their wobble towards the jack.
+1 point for contacting the jack on any turn.
−1 point for contacting any other wobble during the game.
+2 points for capturing the jack (surrounding it with your wobble).
No scores less than zero.

Order of the first throw: ROY G BIV (colors of the rainbow). Order of second throws and beyond: wobble that is farthest away from the jack. Continue until someone captures the jack, finishing that round.

To make your own Wobble game, you will need:
One piece of 1.5-inch diameter PVC tubing × 1.5 inches long (the jack)
Six pieces of 3-inch diameter PVC tubing × 3 inches long, painted (the wobbles)
Six clothespins of the same color as the wobbles (score pins)
One 12-inch ruler (score keeper)

"To invent, you need a good imagination and a pile of junk."

—Thomas A. Edison

I like to invent stuff, especially if what I invent turns out to be fun. While cleaning out my wood shop this summer, I found a few random pieces of large diameter PVC tubing. When I tried cutting these pieces on my band saw, the blade wandered and the result was erratic. I tossed one of these pieces out the door of my workshop, and it wobbled across my lawn as it rolled. Not a very smooth roller I decided, but then thought better of my judgment. Maybe it was not supposed to roll smoothly, and that was how Wobble came to be. You can find directions for making your own Wobble game at the *Teamwork & Teamplay* website (www.teamworkandteamplay.com), and you can purchase a Wobble kit (and tons of other great teambuilding resources, books, and props) by contacting Jim Cain at: jimcain@teamworkandteamplay.com, and asking for his Experiential Garage Sale list.

77. MAGIC CARPET

Magic Carpet is a teambuilding activity that encourages community and connection by inviting people to work together in a small space. You'll need a tarp (or plastic tablecloth) to make a magic carpet for each group of 8 to 12 people. Invite the group to stand completely on the magic carpet and then to flip over the magic carpet without lifting people up and with no one touching the floor or ground.

Most groups attempt to roll or fold and then twist the magic carpet until they can reach the other side. I like to conduct this activity with several small magic carpets rather than a single large one. Multiple magic carpets enable a solution unavailable if you use only a single magic carpet: cooperation between groups.

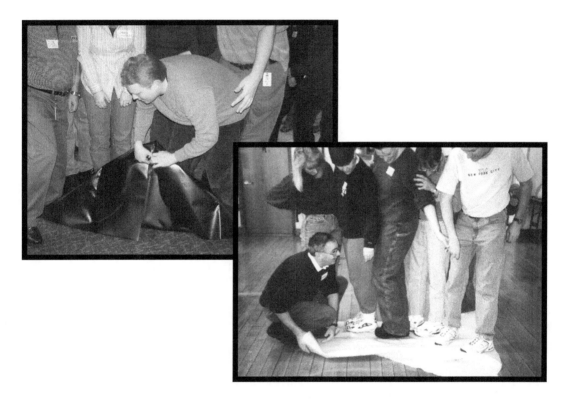

To make Magic Carpet an even more valuable activity, supply masking tape and pens so that participants can write personal goals on one side of the magic carpet and the obstacles or barriers to achieving these goals on the other side. Then invite everyone to share their goals aloud, and their barriers, too. Then have the group mount the magic carpet (on the barrier side) and turn it over to reach their goals.

You can purchase a very durable Magic Carpet from www.training-wheels.com and use this same equipment for other games in this book, such as: Sunny Side Up and the Tarp Jump.

78. A PERFECT MATCH

The equipment for the *Teamwork & Teamplay* activity *A Perfect Match* is a collection of 12 similar objects. Two of these objects are exact duplicates (twins) of each other. Blindfolded participants are asked to determine which two pieces are identical. Each participant is given one piece. They can feel the shape and discuss what they have in their hands, but they cannot pass the piece to anyone else, or touch anyone else's shape. If requested, the facilitator can identify the color of the piece held by any participant. This activity will generally take 10 to 20 minutes for a group to complete. Up to 12 people can participate. Additional participants can act as observers and then share their observations during the debriefing component of this activity. In order to complete this communication activity, participants must use precise language and identify key differences in each of the objects they hold.

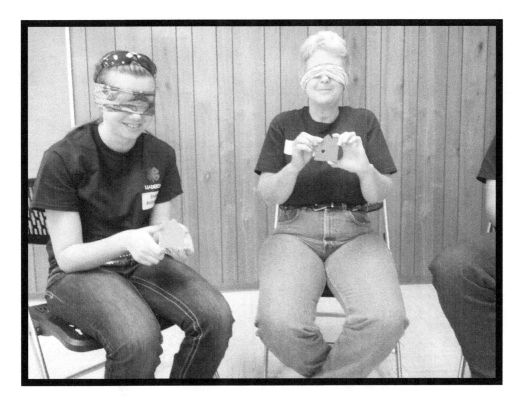

You can make your own collection of Perfect Match objects using toys, plastic shapes, and other simple objects. You can also use wooden shapes available at most craft stores. *A Perfect Match* kits and instructions are available from www.teamworkandteamplay.com.

79. BLIND TRUST DRIVE

The Blind Trust Drive is my favorite activity for exploring and building trust with a partner. The front partner (the driver) closes their eyes, and the backseat partner (the GPS unit) helps the driver navigate safely. After a few minutes, partners switch positions and the activity continues.

After each round of the Blind Trust Drive, I like to include a feedback session so that the driver can tell their GPS unit what they did well and how they might improve.

Be sure to tell participants (especially younger audiences) that this is not a demolition derby. This is not bumper cars. The goal of this activity is zero contact with other drivers or boundaries (walls) in the area. And why do you want to be an excellent backseat driver? Because halfway through when the facilitator says "Switch," your partner is going to remember how you treated them.

Encourage the front seat driver to keep their hands on the (imaginary) wheel. This is a good safety position for the front driver, protecting them from contact with other drivers in the area. The backseat driver keeps both hands on their partner's shoulders, verbally and physically helping to steer them away from traffic jams and other obstacles.

During a corporate teambuilding program I facilitated the Blind Trust Drive activity. One member of the group was legally blind, sensing only light and darkness, but little else. During the first half of this activity, the truly blind person was in front and navigated perfectly with the aid of his sighted partner. But when I instructed the group to switch, I noticed that the blind person was now the GPS system in the back. I asked the new front seat driver if he was okay with this arrangement, and he assured me that he had complete faith in his back seat driver. That vote of confidence created great trust and respect between those two partners, and even better, the second round was just as successful as the first!

80. PETECAS

The Peteca is a Brazilian hand shuttlecock game that is often played in a very competitive way. For the purpose of building unity, community, and connection, here is a slightly less competitive version of the game. Begin with a group of about 10 people standing in a circle. Introduce the game to the group by passing a Peteca around the circle so that everyone can feel the size and weight of the Peteca. Demonstrate hitting the Peteca into the air, palms up (like a volleyball). Then invite the group to keep the Peteca in the air for a total of at least 21 hits. Ready, go!

After a few minutes of play, invite the group to stop and discuss what is currently going well in the group and what needs to be changed to succeed. Then continue playing for a few more minutes, before introducing some alternative ways of playing.

Some of my favorite variations of Peteca include: using only your non-dominant hand, using either hand but only standing on one foot, clapping three times after hitting the Peteca, touching the floor after hitting the Peteca, turning around (360 degrees) after hitting the Peteca, giving your neighbor a high-five after each hit, rotating the circle to the left and playing while moving, saying your name as you hit the Peteca, counting by the alphabet (A through Z) instead of counting by numbers, and then instead of saying a letter of the alphabet saying the name of a food (or animal) that begins with that letter (Apple, Banana, Cookie, Doughnut, etc.). With so many variations, you can easily use this activity to explore adapting to change, change management, and other issues related to dealing with change.

Petecas typically work best for players that are 10 years or older. For younger audiences or anyone with limited mobility or eye-hand coordination, try playing these same variations using a beach ball or a large balloon.

Bill Henderson of Lima, Ohio, introduced me to what he called a Funderbird nearly four decades ago. Bill makes Funderbirds by hand, turning the wood spools on a lathe in his woodworking shop and often using real leather for the base. I later found out that Brazilians know this item as a Peteca, and it is a very popular sport in South America. For more information about the Peteca, you can find an extensive 20-page article on the *Teamwork & Teamplay* website (www.teamworkandteamplay.com/resources.html). Look for the PDF entitled "The Featherball."

You can purchase Petecas and many other great teambuilding props from Training Wheels, Inc. (www.training-wheels.com), or make your own using instructions found in the book *Teamwork & Teamplay* (ISBN 978-0-7872-4532-0) by Jim Cain and Barry Jolliff.

81. THE BOBSLED TEAM

In this no-prop teambuilding activity, trains of four people trade places when specific commands are issued. Metaphorically, these four people represent a bobsled team, and the activity facilitator is their coach.

Begin the activity with multiple groups of four people standing in a line, hands on the shoulders of the person in front of them. Then listen for each of the following commands, and perform the task required:

Command	Action
Change	The person in position one moves to position four.
Switch	The people in position two and position three trade places.
Rotate	Everyone turns around (180 degrees) and faces the other way.

In Round One (the practice round), invite each bobsled team to perform the above basic commands when commanded by their coach (facilitator). Then begin to stack two or three commands together. Next, give each group two minutes to work together and practice these commands on their own.

In Round Two (the semi-finals), continue to stack even more commands together, increasing the speed at which bobsled members need to change places.

In Round Three (the championship round), compliment each team on making it to the final competition, but tell them that in this round, there is one more command. When coaches (facilitators) yell "Loose Caboose," bobsled team members are to scatter and quickly form brand new teams of four players.

I first witnessed a version of this activity when Chris Cavert and Sam Sikes shared it during a pre-conference workshop at the ACCT conference in San Antonio, Texas. I previously called this activity The Change Train until I saw Michelle Cummings teach this activity using the bobsled metaphor. Thanks Sam, Chris, and Michelle for sharing the good stuff! The Bobsled Team is now my favorite no prop teambuilding activity.

If you enjoy this style of no-prop teambuilding activity, you can find many more in the book *Find Something To Do* by Jim Cain (ISBN 978-0-9882046-0-7) available from Healthy Learning (www.healthylearning.com) and Training Wheels, Inc. (www.training-wheels.com).

If you enjoy the Bull Ring Community, there are several other variations of this activity featured in the book *Rope Games* by Jim Cain (ISBN 978-0-9882046-1-4) available from Healthy Learning (www.healthylearning.com) and Training Wheels, Inc. (www.training-wheels.com). Training Wheels, Inc. also sells two other versions of the Bull Ring activity, a three-dimensional PVC tube version and a hooked block version called Goin' Fishin'. The PVC candelabra pictured here is made from Teamplay Tubes, created by Jim Cain and available from Training Wheels.

82. BULL RING COMMUNITY

A Bull Ring is a very simple but powerful teambuilding prop consisting of a metal ring and 12 colorful strings. The challenge is to transport a tennis ball using this device without dropping it.

I like to set my participants up for success by giving each of them the opportunity to practice using the Bull Ring before issuing higher levels of challenge. First, I place a tennis ball on each Bull Ring and ask each group to lower the ball onto a plastic spool (stand), shown in the photographs on the opposite page. Then I ask them to lift the ball and then lower it again to the stand. Next, I ask them to lift the ball, rotate their group half way (180 degrees), close one eye, and return the ball to the stand. Finally, I ask each of three groups to lift the ball, change places with other groups, and place the ball on a new stand, but all three groups must touch down at exactly the same time. Once groups have completed these warm-up Bull Ring activities, they are ready for the final challenge: the Bull Ring Community.

The goal of the Bull Ring Community is for three teams (up to 36 people total) to pick up their tennis balls and then relocate them to a PVC candelabra (shown here) placing all three balls down at the same time. This task sometimes creates a traffic jam as groups position themselves around the final destination.

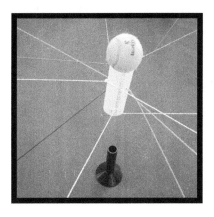

100 Activities That Build Unity, Community & Connection • Jim Cain

Here are a few additional word circles that I created while flying from Phoenix to Charlotte recently:

3 Cards	Switch – Yard – Light (switch yard, yard light, light switch)
5 Cards	Office – Party – Time – Out – Post
5 Cards	Board – Foot – Ball – Game – Over
6 Cards	Time – Travel – Log – Book – Shelf – Life
6 Cards	River – Bank – Note – Book – Mark – Down
8 Cards	Race – Car – Seat – Belt – Buckle – Up – River – Rat
8 Cards	Time – Out – Side – Line – Art – Work – Shop – Rag
11 Cards	Book – Smart – Car – Pool – Table – Setting – Down – Play – Time – Travel – Guide
14 Cards	Front – Door – Man – Power – Lunch – Break – Down – Play – Time – Off – Key – Chain – Lightning – Storm
16 Cards	Ring – Tone – Up – Swing – Set – Down – Play – Ball – Game – Day – Light – Work – Out – Cast – Off – Key
20 Cards	Off – Road – Way – Back – Seat – Warmer – Weather – Channel – Guide – Book – Shelf – Life – Guard – Fence – Post – Game – Over – Time – Out – Take
21 Cards	Spring – Break – Fast – Pace – Car – Wash – Day – Dream – Team – Work – Week – End – Note – Book – Store – Front – Yard – Light – Sleeper – Sofa – Bed
24 Cards	Trip – Wire – Frame – Work – Out – Cast – Off – Line – Art – Show – Place – Setting – Down – Field – Goal – Post – Office – Party – City – Scape – Goat – Farm – House – Boat

83. WORD CIRCLES

Word Circles are a linguistic puzzle for teams. Individual words are written on separate index cards and groups are challenged to rearrange these cards to create combinations (word pairs) that not only make sense, but also create a complete circle of words. For example, the following seven words can be rearranged to make a complete word circle with the following word pairs: team work, work week, week end, end game, game day, day dream, dream team.

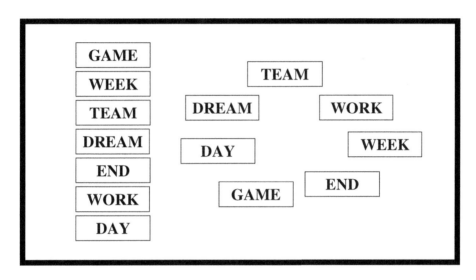

Some combinations of word pairs "work," but if they do not complete the circle, they are not the correct combination.

In addition to the actual word cards used in Word Circles, I like to add three additional "help cards" for the group to use as they deem necessary. As the number of word cards increase, from 7 to 20 or even 30, these help cards become very valuable resources. Typical help cards are:

Chris Cavert and Chip Schlegel are the creative minds behind the linguistic puzzles known as Word Circles. You can find a dozen of these puzzles in Chris's book *Portable Teambuilding Activities* (ISBN 978-1-939019-14-1) available from www.wnbpub.com.

84. SPIRAL WALK

A trust walk with a purpose!

The Spiral Walk is a very simple activity for partners, which explores communication and trust. First, invite partners to create a spiral labyrinth on the floor, using a rope or masking tape. Then place an object at the center of the spiral, such as a tennis ball, trinket, or something of value to the participants. Next, one person closes their eyes, and their sighted partner offers verbal commands to help them walk to the center of the labyrinth without touching the rope or tape boundary of the spiral. After retrieving the object at the center, the sighted partner again helps their sightless partner navigate back out of the spiral labyrinth with verbal commands. Anyone making it to the center of the spiral, recovering the object placed there, and returning to the start without touching the boundary rope or tape of the spiral gets to keep the object they recover!

As an alternative to verbal communication, sighted partners can "communicate" by placing their hands on the shoulders of their sightless partner and steer them through the spiral labyrinth.

This simple activity encourages partners to develop clear communication and also builds trust as partners learn to work together.

If you choose to use masking tape to create your Spiral Labyrinth, I suggest using the blue painter's tape, which sticks well but is much easier to remove than standard masking or duct tape.

CHAPTER 4

Debriefing Techniques & Closing Activities

This chapter contains over a dozen activities for actively reviewing with your group and concluding your program.

No.	Activity Name	Teachable Moment	Ideal Group Size
85	Shuffle Left / Shuffle Right	Active Reviewing Technique	10 or More People
86	The Virtual Slideshow	Imaginary Images	Any
87	A Circle of Connection	Connection	10+ per Group
88	A Circle of Kindness	Empathy, Connection	10 or More People
89	The Four-Minute Team	Creative Closing	Teams of 4 People
90	Closing Stories	Closing Thoughts	Any
91	Closing Songs	Musical Endings	20 or More People
92	The Last Dance	Active Closings	20 or More People
93	Making Connections	Connection	20 or More People
94	An Attitude of Gratitude	Saying Thank You	Any
95	The One Ball That Does It All	Debriefing Technique	Any
96	The UFO Ball / The Energy Stick	A Visual/Auditory Closing	Any
97	The Learning Rope	Memory Technique	Any
98	Pass the Knot	Debriefing Technique	Any
99	Three for the Road	Memory Technique	Any
100	Thumbprints	Visual Debriefing Tools	Any

85. SHUFFLE LEFT / SHUFFLE RIGHT

This simple reviewing technique has two outstanding qualities. First, it is active, which keeps your group moving and engaged. Second, it creates a space for even the quietest voice to be heard.

At the completion of a teambuilding activity, invite your group to create a circle surrounding the props just used in your activity. Then instruct everyone to shuffle (side step) to the left around the circle. At some point, say, "Stop" and explain to the group when someone says stop, the group stops and listens to the person issuing the command. When that person finishes talking, they tell the group to "Shuffle left" or "Shuffle right" and the group begins moving again until another stop command is issued.

I like to frame this activity with general reviewing questions, such as, "Tell me about your group's performance in this activity," rather than more specific ones. This allows a great number of people to participate as they interpret the question through their own experience.

Continue this activity until the group makes a complete circle with no one saying stop.

I've noticed that in some groups when participants sit down they shut down. Shuffle Left / Shuffle Right is an active debriefing technique that keeps the group moving and engaged. I also know that some participants think more quickly than others. Groups sometime circle almost completely around before someone in the group speaks up. As a facilitator, you should be comfortable with silence. Don't feel that you have to fill that space. Someone in your group will do it for you!

86. THE VIRTUAL SLIDESHOW

The Virtual Slideshow is my absolute favorite debriefing activity. To begin this reviewing technique, invite the members of your group to close their eyes and remember the events of the day. Ask them to mentally take a photograph of their favorite activity or moment. Then, when they have a photo in mind, open their eyes. This "closed eye" technique will allow the facilitator to see when everyone in the group has identified a photograph. When everyone has their eyes open, you can continue with the activity.

Present the group with a Virtual Slideshow "clicker," a simple plastic debriefing tool that makes a clicking sound when the metal insert is pressed. This sound mimics the sound of the old-fashioned 35mm slide projector clickers, the newer computer project slideshow clicker, or even your TV's remote control. Then invite everyone to show their imaginary photograph(s) from the day (by clicking the clicker) and narrate what is happening in the photo. When finished, encourage the speaker to just ask, "Who would like the clicker next?"

The Virtual Slideshow is an excellent way to encourage participants to share more information during a debriefing or reviewing session. Once they have a picture in mind, it is an easy task to talk about the content of the photo at length.

I originally learned the Virtual (or imaginary) Slideshow debriefing activity from Bea Cleveland of the state 4-H office at The Ohio State University. Bea used the word virtual before we even had home computers!

A teacher informed me that the Virtual Slideshow incorporates all three major forms of education. It is auditory because you can hear the clicking sound and the narration. It is kinesthetic because it requires manual manipulation, and it is visual even though the image is imaginary.

You can find slide show "clickers" for this activity from www.training-wheels.com and also at many pet stores (they are also used to train dogs).

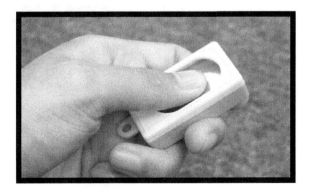

87. A CIRCLE OF CONNECTION

The things which connect us bring us a little bit closer together.

This simple closing activity will leave the people in each small group well connected. One member of the group begins by introducing themselves to the group and standing with their hands on their hips, elbows out. This person mentions specific things they enjoyed about the program or event. The first person in the group who agrees with them links elbows with them. This second person then continues to mention significant things they enjoyed, and another person links to them. The activity continues until all members of the group have linked together. The final task is for the last person to continue sharing until the first person can link to them, at which point everyone in the group will be standing connected in a small circle.

Thanks to Dick Hammond of Texas for sharing this wonderfully connective closing activity. You can find many other excellent activities in the book *The Empty Bag* by Dick Hammond and Chris Cavert (ISBN 978-0-9746-4421-8) available from Training Wheels, Inc. (www.training-wheels.com).

88. A CIRCLE OF KINDNESS

The formation for this closing activity is two concentric circles, with everyone facing toward the center. One half of the group forms the inner circle. The second half of the group forms the outer circle, with one member of the outer circle standing behind each member of the inner circle, gently placing both hands on their partner's shoulders.

Members of the inside circle close their eyes, and the outer circle has the opportunity to express a positive comment (whisper) to their inside circle partner. Typical comments might include, "It was great meeting you, and I am looking forward to working with you. Thanks for your help with the problem solving activity." This activity however is not a two-way conversation; the only response possible from the inner circle is "Thank you." This avoids breaking the mood with laughter, giggling, or any other fun but disruptive conversation.

After the outer circle has completed a full revolution, they change places with their inner circle partner and the activity continues.

You can find this activity and more than a dozen more no-prop debriefing and closing activities in the book *Find Something to Do* (ISBN 978-0-9882046-0-7) by Jim Cain, available from Healthy Learning (www.healthylearning.com) and Training Wheels, Inc. (www.training-wheels.com). For even more activities for processing, debriefing, reviewing, and reflection see *A Teachable Moment* (ISBN 978-0-7575-1782-2) by Jim Cain, Michelle Cummings, and Jennifer Stanchfield available from the sources above and Kendall Hunt Publishing (www.kendallhunt.com).

89. THE FOUR-MINUTE TEAM

Here is an interesting closing activity that lends itself to groups of any size. It is best to start this activity with group members scattered about the area and specifically not standing in a circle, line, or other regular formation.

> *"Everyone knows that the ultimate test of teamwork is for a team to hold their arms in the air* (demonstrate, with arms stretched out horizontally, parallel with the ground) *for four minutes. It is almost impossible for anyone to do this without teamwork. Let's see how good of a team you've become. Ready, begin!"* At this point, the facilitator starts a stopwatch.

It can be extremely uncomfortable to hold your arms stretched outward for four minutes. But, by placing your arms on the shoulders of other team members, the challenge becomes easier for everyone! This simple solution is both a neat trick and a great metaphor for teamwork.

You can find this activity and many more no-prop activities in the book *Find Something to Do* (ISBN 978-0-9882046-0-7) by Jim Cain, available from Healthy Learning (www.healthylearning.com) and Training Wheels, Inc. (www.training-wheels.com).

> Here are a few of my favorite closing stories.
>
> *Little World: A Book About Tolerance* (ISBN 978-0-9715-3335-0) by Joanna Carolan
>
> *Everybody Needs a Rock* (ISBN 978-0-6897-1051-8) by Birdie Baylor
>
> *Sir Kevin of Devon* (ISBN 978-1-1272-4014-2) by Adelaide Holl
>
> *Jacob the Baker* (ISBN 978-0-3453-6662-X) by Noah benShea
>
> *All I Really Need to Know I Learned in Kindergarten and The Mermaid in the book All I Really Need to Know I Learned in Kindergarten – 15th Anniversary Edition* (ISBN 978-0-3454-6617-9) by Robert Fulghum.
>
> *Not Even Chickens and The Meaning of Life* by Robert Fulghum in the book What on Earth Have I Done (ISBN 978-0-3123-6549-3) Or better yet, let Robert Fulghum read it to you in his own words, in the audio version of these books.
>
> The story-song *Old City Bar* by the Trans-Siberian Orchestra on the *Christmas Eve and Other Stories* album
>
> *The Syballine Books* read by Douglas Adams on the *Last Chance to See* recording

---

You can find the wooden shapes shown here at www.training-wheels.com. With these shapes, you can facilitate not only this activity, but also a very powerful communication activity.

The Chip and Dan Heath book *Making Ideas Stick: Why Some Ideas Survive and Others Die* (ISBN 978-1-4000-6428-1) details the SUCCESS model. If the content of your program is Simple, Unexpected, Concrete, Credible, Emotional, and involves Significant Stories, it is most likely going to be successful. Have you considered using stories in your programs?

90. CLOSING STORIES

I first started incorporating stories into my programs when my friend and colleague Kirk Weisler suggested including a story with one of my teambuilding activities. For years, I had been using a collection of wooden pieces as my final closing activity with groups. In this collection, there were a variety of shapes and colors. Participants each took a piece without looking at them and then attempted to "find their people" while holding these wooden pieces behind their backs. In this collection, most wooden shapes had at least five similar shapes, but there was only a single wooden star. While other groups were uniting, the star person was typically left alone. After a minute or two of searching, I asked everyone to lock their feet in position and then look at the piece of wood they had. I then invited everyone with a green piece to hold it up. These are some of "your people" even if they are not exactly the same shape. The similarity here was color. Then I asked the star person to tell the group what responses they had when they tried to join a group. You could feel the concern in the room as participants empathized with the star person. Everyone knows the drama of wanting to be part of a group, but perhaps not being invited or not fitting in. I then ask the group what one thing they all had in common (each piece was made of wood). If you can find something in common with everyone, then everyone can be one of "your people."

Kirk Weisler suggested that I tell the Robert Fulghum story *The Mermaid* at the closing of this activity. From the very first time I did, it was an incredible success. So now I invite you to do the same by incorporating some stories of your choosing into your programs. Throughout this book, I've attempted to incorporate stories into each of the activity descriptions. I believe they make the narrative more powerful. You should try it, too!

When I'm on My Journey (Traditional Appalachian Folk Tune)

This is an Appalachian Highlands song that dates back more than 100 years. When settlers from that region continued their journeys west, or when family members concluded their time here on earth, this song was sung not as a sad lament, but as a joyful sendoff to those that were traveling on. It is especially beautiful with harmony.

Chorus
When I'm on my journey,
don't you weep after me
When I'm on my journey,
don't you weep after me
When I'm on my journey,
don't you weep after me
I don't want you to weep after me

Verses
High up on the mountain,
leave your troubles down below
High up on the mountain,
leave your troubles down below
High up on the mountain,
leave your troubles down below
I don't want you to weep after me

Every lonely river must
flow down to the sea
Every lonely river must
flow down to the sea
Every lonely river must
flow down to the sea
I don't want you to weep after me

When the stars are falling
and the thunder starts to roll
When the stars are falling
and the thunder starts to roll
When the stars are falling
and the thunder starts to roll
I don't want you to weep after me

Oh How Lovely Is the Evening (Traditional Folk Tune With Choreography)

This song is not only a beautiful closing tune, but has a very nice bit of choreography as well. Start with three concentric circles of singers. The inner circle should have at least 15 people, with more in the next circle, and still more in the final outer circle. Begin by teaching the lyrics and then teach the choreography (shown to the right of each lyric).

The beauty in this song emerges when it is sung as a round. The inner circle begins by holding hands and moving counterclockwise (to the right), when they reach the second line of the verse, they reverse directions and move clockwise (to the left) and the second circle begins the first line, moving to the right, while holding hands. When the inner circle finished the second line of the verse, they stand still and swing their arms slowly forward and back, while singing the "ding dong" portion of the lyrics. At the same time, the middle circle begins moving to the left (clockwise) and the outer circle starts the song, moving to the right (counterclockwise). Repeat the song three times. When the inner circle reaches the "ding dong" part for the last time, they keep singing "ding dong" until all three circles are done. Finish with the entire group holding the last word with their joined hands raised upward.

Lyrics	Choreography
Oh how lovely is the evening, is the evening	Walk counterclockwise (to the right)
When the bells are sweetly ringing, sweetly ringing	Walk clockwise (to the left)
Ding, dong, ding, dong, ding, dong	Stand still, facing the center, and swing arms forward on "ding" and backward on "dong."

91. CLOSING SONGS

One of my favorite ways to conclude a conference or workshop is singing in circles. Even ordinary songs become extraordinary when a hundred or more voices in close proximity join together in song. Maybe it is because of all the closing ceremonies I attended at 4-H camps over the years or perhaps because of the song-leading qualities of Bill Henderson at the Buckeye Leadership Workshop that I appreciate this style of group singing. Make no mistake, this style of singing in circles and just the right song will create a very powerful and memorable closing experience.

Start by inviting your audience to join hands and form three concentric circles. Then place yourself at the center of the group and lead them in song. In this position, you'll be at the center of a tremendous amount of vocal energy. Trust me when I say that you'll never experience a more powerful singing experience than this.

Two of my favorite closing songs are presented on the opposite page. MP3 song files of these two songs, sung by the Buckeye Leadership Workshop alumni, are available for free at the Teamwork & Teamplay website: www.teamworkandteamplay.com/resources.html. You can also purchase three different musical CD recordings by BLW featuring these songs and many more sing-able tunes. For more information, visit: www.buckeyeleadership.org.

In the early days of radio, traveling groups of singers and instrumentalists often performed live. Some of the most talented singers were family groups, and many of these not only stood close to each other in the tight confines of the radio studio, but also maintained physical contact with each other as they sang, so that they were able to feel the vibration of each word as they sang together.

You can download a free PDF document of these closing songs (and many more closing activities) from the Teamwork & Teamplay website. See the document *Building Community with Music, Singing and Dance* by Jim Cain at: www.teamworkandteamplay.com/resources.html

92. THE LAST DANCE

If you don't happen to have an audience that can sing, you can still create a powerful musical experience by incorporating recorded music in your closing activities. I like to include movement with music, so here is my recipe for a unique closing activity.

First, choose a recorded song with lyrics that are meaningful to your audience, and play this at an appropriate volume through an amplified speaker system. Some of my current favorite closing songs include: "Brother" by Lord Huron, "Storms in Africa" by Enya, "Precious" by Melissa Etheridge, "Friends Are Friends Forever" by Michael W. Smith, and the theme song from *The Lion King* soundtrack.

Now it is time to build community. Invite multiple groups of about eight people to gather around a knotted Raccoon Circle, grasp it with both hands, and gently lean back (just a tiny bit), and balance the circle. Then ask them to close their eyes and begin playing the song of your choice.

Finally, we will add some choreography. At some appropriate point in the song, invite each person to open their eyes and holding on with just their left hand, pinwheel to the right (like a giant rotating gear). Participants in each circle can high-five the members of other circles as they pass. Then reverse directions, and everyone can high-five going the other way. This is a great way for participants to physically connect with each other during the closing ceremony.

Raccoon Circles are 15-foot (4.6 meters) long segments of tubular climbing webbing knotted into a circle. You can find this activity and almost 200 more in *The Revised and Expanded Book of Raccoon Circles* (ISBN 978-0-7575-3265-8) by Jim Cain and Tom Smith, available from Healthy Learning (www.healthylearning.com) and Training Wheels, Inc. (www.training-wheels.com). You can also download a free PDF document of Raccoon Circle activities from the Teamwork & Teamplay website at: www.teamworkandteamplay.com/resources.html.

93. MAKING CONNECTIONS

Here is a beautiful technique for physically connecting your audience during a closing activity. Begin this closing activity with participants close enough to see and touch each other but with enough space leftover to allow movement when necessary. Next, introduce some of the phrases below to your audience and invite them to Make Connections with people in the group that embody a particular phrase.

Make a connection with someone that:

has taught you something of great value – keeps working even when others quit – has shown you great kindness – has made you feel welcome – has shared a meal with you – you aspire to be more like – has been a mentor to you – you want to know better – has befriended you – has made you laugh – encourages you – you care about – inspires you – respects you – demonstrates caring.

For an even more powerful (and anonymous) experience, try this activity with half of the audience standing with their eyes closed and the other half moving about and making connections when appropriate. Then switch roles so that everyone has the opportunity to be on both the receiving and connecting side.

Take into account the culture of your audience and suggest culturally appropriate techniques for Making Connections with each other, such as shaking hands, placing hands on shoulders, or even just pointing to each other (a non-contact technique).

I learned a variation of this activity from Faith Evans, who has several books, including *Grab and Go Activities* (I and II) and *Play It, Measure It*, all available from Healthy Learning (www.healthylearning.com).

94. AN ATTITUDE OF GRATITUDE

Gratitude: The Quality of Being Thankful

Gratitude affects not only the person receiving it, but the person giving it as well. By simply reflecting on gratitude in your life, the positive effects of this reflection can last for days. Leave time at the end of your next program for participants to express their gratitude to each other, to the event organizers, to anyone they would like. This gratitude can be expressed verbally or written down on index cards or in dozens of creative ways of your choosing. Visit Pinterest for some truly amazing and artistic ways to express thankfulness and gratitude.

In the book *59 Seconds*, Richard Wiseman reveals that having people list three things that they are grateful for in their life or to reflect on three events that have gone especially well recently can significantly increase their level of happiness for about a month. This, in turn, can cause them to be more optimistic about the future and can improve their physical health.

I have had the opportunity to visit more than thirty 30 countries so far, and one of the first things I try to learn when I visit a new country is how to say hello and thank you in the local dialect. With only these two phrases, you'd be surprised how easy it is to connect with people around the world. Next time you travel to a foreign country, try learning these two phrases before you arrive.

95. THE ONE BALL THAT DOES IT ALL

For this debriefing activity, you will need a ball and a few index cards. Begin by writing a dozen sequential numbers onto a ball with a permanent marker. Next, you will need to write a dozen questions on an index card specific to the theme of your reviewing session. If leadership is the major theme, most of your questions should explore leadership topics and issues.

Then toss the ball to various participants in your group. The person catching the ball identifies the number closest to their right thumb and then answers the question associated with this number on the index card.

Question cards are prepared in advance and can be for a variety of topics, from leadership to teamwork to communication to debriefing or reviewing, such as: *What leadership talents do you find most helpful in a group setting?* or *How did you define success in this activity?* or *List three things that could have made your group more effective in this activity*. A spiral-bound set of index cards is a simple way to keep track of your multiple-theme question cards. You can invite one of your participants to read the questions, effectively inviting the group to control their own reviewing session.

Another creative debriefing tool is known as a Thumball produced by the company Answers in Motion. Thumballs are the award-winning creation of Gregg Pembleton. These creative products come in a variety of sizes, content, and languages, including: icebreakers, leadership, communication, conflict resolution, movement, the alphabet, numbers, and creative debriefing questions. You can even customize your own design. Visit www.thumball.com for more information.

You'll find this activity and over a hundred more ideas for processing, debriefing, reviewing, and reflection in the book *A Teachable Moment* (ISBN 978-0-7575-1782-2) by Jim Cain, Michelle Cummings, and Jennifer Stanchfield, available from www.healthylearning.com and www.kendallhunt.com.

96. THE UFO BALL / THE ENERGY STICK

For those of you that like STEM (Science, Technology, Engineering, and Math), here is a closing activity that actually measures the connectedness of your group. You will need one of the devices shown below, which are available in science stores and at www.training-wheels.com. The UFO Ball and the Energy Stick are science toys that produce sound and light when a closed circuit is created.

I like to begin this activity by showing the UFO Ball or Energy Stick and demonstrating that by touching both ends (making a complete circuit with my body), the device can be activated. Then I ask for a volunteer from the audience to join hands with me and touch one contact on the device with one of their hands while I touch the other contact with my hand, producing another closed circuit and lighting the device. Then I invite everyone in the audience to try this with us. Simply by joining hands most groups are able to create a closed circuit. I have successfully done this activity with 60 people, and if you use several balls, even larger groups are possible. For the most dramatic effect, try using these devices in low lighting and with a microphone to amplify the sound emitted.

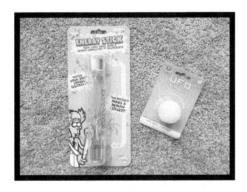

A neat variation (and one that teaches your audience about electrical polarity) is to invite your audience to simultaneously light up four UFO balls in a single circle of people. They will need to orient all four balls or sticks correctly (matching polarity) to accomplish this technical feat of connectedness.

Juan Mario Gutierrez of Kajuyali Camps invited me to Bogota, Colombia to train his summer camp staff. On my first visit, I happened to bring a UFO ball with me. At the very end of the training, I produced the ball, circled my group, and ... nothing happened! This particular day, all the counselors were barefooted, standing on a humid concrete floor. Their connection with the floor short-circuited the UFO ball completely. So, a valuable lesson here. These devices work best if your participants are insulated (via their shoes) from the floor.

You can purchase UFO Balls and The Energy Stick (also called the Sci-Fi Tube) from www.training-wheels.com

97. THE LEARNING ROPE

Here is a brilliant way to help your next group remember all the teachable moments experienced during a training program. You will need a rope about 10 feet (3 meters) long.

Throughout the program, each time *a teachable moment* is experienced, a member of the group ties a single knot onto the learning rope. Before a new knot is added, the group reviews all previous knots to ensure that the learning is not lost. At the end of the day, untie each knot as the group identifies and reflects on each teachable moment or cut the rope between each knot and send the members of your group home with a reminder of the teachable moments they experienced.

This is an excellent technique for reinforcing the learning in your program and helping your group to remember the most important moments of the day.

Thanks to Chris Cavert for sharing this helpful reviewing technique. It is without a doubt one of the most valuable things I ever learned to do with a piece of rope. You can find even more great ideas on Chris's blog at www.fundoing.com. For even more simple but profound ways to use rope as part of your teambuilding program, see the book *Rope Games* (ISBN 978-0-9882-0461-4) available from www.healthylearning.com and www.training-wheels.com.

Mariners in the Pacific Islands historically used knotted ropes as an early form of navigational map. The size of a knot denoted the relative size of an island, fishing grounds, or landmark, and the distance between knots was proportional to the distance required to row or sail between these places.

98. PASS THE KNOT

Here is a final reviewing technique I like to use with my entire audience. You'll need one long rope for this activity, sufficient in length so that everyone in the group can grasp the rope at the same time. Begin by inviting everyone in your group to grasp the rope. Then begin to pass the knot (which ties the rope into a circle) slowly to the right. The knot is rather like a "talking stick" in this activity. Invite anyone that would like to speak to wait until the knot is directly in their grasp and then say "Stop." This is their opportunity to speak. After they have finished, the knot is again passed around the circle and continues moving until another person stops the knot in order to share their thoughts.

Be sure to allow the knot two complete revolutions of the circle near the end of this activity. Some participants require plenty of thinking time and silence before they are ready to share with the group.

You can make the perfect size debriefing rope for this activity by knotting together multiple Raccoon Circles or using a single, long piece of rope. For more debriefing activities using rope, see Roger Greenaway's outstanding website at www.reviewing.co.uk and the book *Rope Games* (ISBN 978-0-9882-0461-4) by Jim Cain, available from www.healthylearning.com and www.training-wheels.com.

99. THREE FOR THE ROAD

No doubt most audiences are exposed to plenty of valuable things during your teaching and training programs. Unfortunately, it is unlikely that they will be able to remember everything you have presented. Three for the Road is an attempt to have each person focus on the three most significant or valuable insights of the day by writing these on a colorful index card and then placing this card in a highly visible location after the conclusion of the program.

At the end of your program, pass out index cards and pens to your audience and allow each person to write down the three most significant things they have learned that day. Invite each person to find a partner or form a small group and share the three things they have written on their card. Then invite each person to share how they plan to use this information in the future. These simple techniques increase the possibility that your participants will take the valuable information you have shared and make use of it in their world.

According to Edgar Dale's Cone of Learning, the greater the interaction of the learner with the material, the greater the retention of that information. By writing, reading, sharing, and discussing the Three for the Road insights, each participant increases the probability of remembering these valuable lessons.

If you want to read my personal list of Three for the Road insights, see the article *Closing Thoughts* near the last page of this book. There you will find three amazing insights that I love to share with participants in my workshops (and now those reading this book). I hope you are as inspired by these three things as I am.

100. THUMBPRINTS

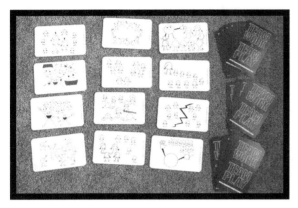

The 12 thumbprints in the Teamwork & Teamplay Training Cards illustrate a variety of team performance situations. Place these images so that they are visible to your group. Then invite participants to interact with these images while discussing the following questions:

1. Place these images in order from best (ideal) team behavior to worst (poorest team behavior).
2. Which images illustrate positive team behavior, and which are negative?
3. Which image most accurately illustrates the present nature of this group right now?
4. Which image is most like this group when things are going well?
5. Which image represents this group under pressure or experiencing conflict?
6. Which thumbprint (circle person) do you most identify with in any given illustration? Why?

The Thumbprints found here and on the Teamwork & Teamplay Training Cards were created by Dave Knobbe. These cards are available from www.healthylearning.com and www.training-wheels.com. Together with Clare Marie Hannon and Jim Cain, Dave is the author of *Essential Staff Training Activities* (ISBN 978-0-7575-6167-2) available from www.healthylearning.com and www.kendallhunt.com.

The Action Pak debriefing cards shown here are the collection of 100 colorful cards, spanning the range of human emotion with images and words, created by Craig Rider. For more information about these cards contact Jim Cain at: jimcain@teamworkandteamplay.com. There are, in fact, many visual debriefing cards available. The *Images of Organizations Toolbox* of cards is available from www.rsvpdesign.co.uk and is one of the best collections of such cards in the world. Soularium cards with a Christian focus are available from www.CruPress.com. *Chiji Processing Cards* by Steve Simpson were some of the original visual debriefing cards, and now there is the *Chiji Guidebook* (ISBN 978-2-8854-7384-4) available from www.wnbpub.com.

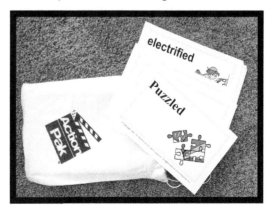

CHAPTER 5

Bonus Activities

This fifth and final chapter contains several bonus activities and room for you to record your own favorite ways to build unity, community, and connection.

No.	Activity Name	Teachable Moment	Ideal Group Size
101	Bonus Activities		
	The Tarp Jump	Split Second Teamwork	10+ per tarp
	A Linguistic Challenge	Tongue Twisting Opener	20 per group
	Popcorn	Problem Solving	20 to 30 people
	TV Theme Songs	Memory / Age Diversity	6 people per group
	The Jump Rope Challenge	Kinesthetic Teamwork	3 to 31 people per group
	Three-Dimensional Bull Ring	Teamwork	12 people per group
	Goin' Fishin'	Teamwork	12 people per group
	Nuts & Bolts	Problem Solving / Teamwork	Multiple Groups of 8
	Lightning Stones	Debriefing Technique	Any
	Thoughts, Words, & Deeds	Resolving Conflict	Any
102	Your Favorite Activities		

101. BONUS ACTIVITIES

When I was first preparing my list of activities to include in this book project, I began with a list of over 200 possibilities. My goal was to refine that list, specifically to those activities that I have witnessed building unity, community, and connection in the groups I have facilitated. But even with those criteria, I still had a few extra activities that I wanted to share, so here they are.

The Tarp Jump
Carefully Timed Teamwork

I featured this activity in my book, the *Teamwork & Teamplay International Edition* (ISBN 978-0-9882046-3-8) because you can create amazing teamwork with just a simple tarp, tablecloth, or blanket. Begin by placing a tarp on the floor, and invite your group to stand on top of it. Next, ask the group to designate one person in their group to be the puller. The challenge is for the group to simply jump straight up into the air, and while they are in the air, for the puller to pull the tarp out from underneath them, so they land on the floor.

This activity explores so many valuable teambuilding skills, such as communication, timing, teamwork, problem solving, creativity, and of course the opportunity to celebrate when the group accomplishes the task.

A Linguistic Challenge
Thank You, Dr. Seuss

For many years, Larry Beatty (the director at Jumonville in Pennsylvania) hosted a spring workshop for adventure-based learning. During one of the pre-conference workshops I presented, one of my participants shared a very interesting vocal warm-up activity using the book *Fox in Socks* by Dr. Seuss (ISBN 978-0-394-80038-7). In our circle of about

20 people, he presented the book, and then handed it to the person next to him to begin reading. The challenge of this activity is for each person to begin reading out loud and continue until they make a mistake, at which point they pass the book along to the next person. The goal is to finish the book before it is passed around the entire circle.

If you like tongue twisters, there is an amazing collection of them (3,660+ entries in 118 languages) at: www.uebersetzung.at. You are invited to also try the TTTT (tongue twister total time) challenge featured in the book *Teambuilding Puzzles* (ISBN 978-0-7575-7040-7) by Mike Anderson, Jim Cain, Chris Cavert, and Tom Heck, available from www.kendallhunt.com and www.healthylearning.com.

Popcorn

Fill an entire room!

Woody Davis, a 4-H Extension Educator, shared this activity with me after a workshop I presented at the Oregon State 4-H Camp. You'll need a bucket filled with various sizes and colors of Wiffle balls (golf balls, baseballs, soft balls) and a well-defined space, such as a classroom or (if you are outside) half a tennis court. Invite your audience to spread out over the entire space available and then lock their feet in place. Next empty the bucket of balls, dispersing them evenly throughout the space. Then place the bucket at the center.

Now challenge your group to gather up all the balls (without moving their feet) and place them into the bucket. Participants are welcome to use any resources within arms reach (such as throwing a shoe at a hard-to-reach ball, or using a belt to swat a ball toward another person in the group). If a few difficult-to-reach balls remain, you can allow each person in the group to keep one foot in contact with the floor, but pivot (like a basketball player) the other foot.

The Jump Rope Challenge

With this activity you can facilitate a group from three people up to 31. Ten pieces of rope, from 1 to 10 feet (30 to 300 cm) in length are presented to the group. Beginning with the shortest rope (1 foot long), each rope must be jumped three consecutive times before the next longer rope can be jumped. The total time required to jump all the ropes is the score. Time begins on the first jump of the shortest rope and concludes with the third jump of the longest rope.

There are three roles in this activity. Participants can be a jumper, a rope twirler, or a timer. Some ropes are long enough for a single person to jump by themselves. The shortest ropes will require two people to twirl the rope and another person to jump it. During each turn, the rope must circumnavigate the jumper (go completely around them). A score time of 45 seconds or less is good. A score time of 30 seconds or less is world class! Encourage participants to find a job that suits their own abilities and that helps the team as a whole.

TV Theme Songs

A Musical Memory Challenge

If you visit your local library, you can often find collections of TV theme songs on CD recordings. Many of these recordings have recent TV shows, but a few also contain the theme songs for 50 years or more of television. If you happen to have a wide age range in your audience, you can use that to your advantage in this activity. Create age-diverse groups of six people and invite them to write down their guesses for each theme song you play. Choose TV shows recent, classic, and ancient. In many cases, your youngest audience members will know the most recent TV shows and your older audience members will remember some older shows.

A Three-Dimensional Bull Ring

A More Challenging Version of Bull Ring

The classic Bull Ring is made from a metal harness ring and 12 strings. It is fairly easy to transport a tennis ball using this device. The 3-D Bull Ring is a bit more challenging. Instead of a metal ring, a three-dimensional PVC tube is used. With this version, it is very easy to tip the tube and drop the ball. If you happen to have a group that has already experienced the Bull Ring activity, you might try this variation instead.

Goin' Fishin'

Another Variation of Bull Ring

I was asked to create a character building team challenge for a pre-school program that had an environmental focus. I created Goin' Fishin' as a variation of the Bull Ring activity, but instead of transporting a tennis ball, I used a familiar wooden block with hooks to pick up wooden fish on which I had written words of character, such as honesty, respect, responsibility, and helpfulness. Students then used this tool to pick up the various fish and then reflect on the words written there.

For some reason, the hook on one of the fish was positioned in just such a way that every time the fish was picked up, it quickly fell off the hooked block. I decided to put the word tenacity on the back of that particular fish.

Goin' Fishin' is a great activity to share with groups that may have already experienced the Bull Ring activity. If you really want to challenge a group, instead of picking up wooden fish or blocks, invite them to pick up a set mousetrap, transport it, and place it down again, without setting it off.

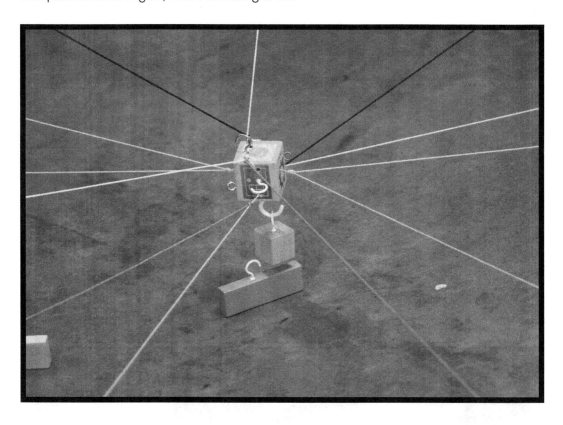

Nuts & Bolts

One of my favorite conferences is the National Challenge Course Practitioner Symposium (now called the Un-Conference) held near Boulder, Colorado, each winter (www.leahy-inc.com). If you ever want to see virtual or open space used effectively, this is the place to do it. Years ago, while attending this conference, John Schultz and Lisa Blockus visited one of Boulder's best hardware stores (www.mcguckin.com) and returned to the conference with a collection of nuts and bolts. They had invented a new teambuilding activity, much like the teambuilding activity Keypunch (or Calculator or Alphabet Soup as some folks call it). The challenge is for a group to correctly assemble (place a nut on each bolt) each of the items present, including: various sizes of nuts and bolts, left-handed threaded bolts and nuts, and a turnbuckle that has one right-hand and one left-hand thread! The total time required is the score. After an initial round, challenge your group to improve their performance time.

Lightning Stones

Lightning Stones or Septarian Nodules are a unique geological formation of clay and siderite (an iron mineral) and exist in only a few places in the entire world. I like to use these stones as a debriefing or reviewing tool. Each stone contains a unique pattern of cracks that remind me of petroglyphs. Pass one of these stones around to each person in your group, and ask them what they "see" in their stone and how this vision relates to the group's performance that day. Consider this an artistic form of reviewing with your group.

    I am told that Lightning Stones only exist in a few places in the world: Russia, New Zealand, and (luckily for me) the southeastern shores of Lake Michigan. If you take a stroll down Pier Cover Beach toward West Side Park, you just may find a few of these very unique stones.

Thoughts, Words, & Deeds

Think About It. Talk About It. Do Something About It.

Building unity, community, and connection is an admirable goal, but this process is sometimes made more difficult when an audience is comprised of people with diverse or even contradictory values, traditions, objectives, and beliefs. If the members of your group say phrases like "us and them" rather than "we," you can use the activities in this book to bridge the gap between these two groups and prepare them to work better together.

The Teamwork & Teamplay website now has a document detailing a new curriculum for building unity, community, and connection with communities in conflict. By thinking, talking, and working together, groups can build a foundation toward existing together in greater harmony. The activities in this book will prepare groups to resolve their conflicts and address their differences from a position of unity.

The activities presented in this book provide a common and meaningful experience for groups and open the door for needed conversations about things that matter. As an example, consider how the following activity demonstrates that each person in the group may have a different point of view.

Remove the numbers (1 through 12) from the clock face of a standard analog (i.e. non-digital) clock and place it on the floor. Then invite your group to circle around the clock and ask each person the very simple question, "According to this clock, what time is it?" Without a common language or a common frame of reference (the numbers), each person has a different point of view and consequently a different answer to the question. In order for all members of the group to agree, the group must decide on a common point of reference, a common framework, a common language.

The lessons learned from each of the activities in this book become small building blocks as a group with opposing views begins to work together. The more activities and teachable moments explored by the group, the greater the number of building blocks created and the greater the potential for resolving conflicts and ultimately working together for the greater good. And what can a group do with these building blocks? They can build what they choose, together!

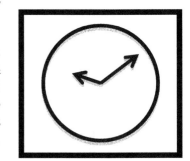

So visit the Teamwork & Teamplay website (www.teamworkandteamplay.com) for the Thoughts, Words, & Deeds curriculum using the activities in this book, and try it the next time you facilitate a program for a group experiencing conflict. Give them the foundational skills they need to begin the process of working well together.

102. YOUR FAVORITE ACTIVITIES

Use these pages to write your own favorite activities for building unity, community, and connection.

REFERENCES, RESOURCES & EQUIPMENT FOR BUILDING UNITY, COMMUNITY & CONNECTION

References

59 Seconds: Think a Little, Change a Lot by Richard Wiseman, 2009, Knopf, New York, NY ISBN 978-0-307-27340-6
Learn the value of reflecting on gratitude from this book.

Connect: 12 Vital Ties That Open Your Heart, Lengthen Your Life and Deepen Your Soul by Edward M. Hallowell, 1999, Pantheon Books, New York, NY ISBN 0-375-40357-4
One of the first books to show substantial data on the value of connection.

Linked: How Everything Is Connected to Everything Else and What It Means for Business, Science, and Everyday Life by Albert-Laszlo Barabasi, 2003, Plume Books, New York, NY ISBN 0-452-28439-2
A scientific approach to the study of connection.

Vital Friends: The People You Can't Afford to Live Without by Tom Rath, 2006, Gallup Press, New York, NY ISBN 978-1-59562-007-1
This book contains some amazing statistics related to the value of building relationships at work.

When Strangers Meet: How People You Don't Know Can Transform You by Kio Stark, 2016, TED Books ISBN 978-1-5011-1998-9
Talking to strangers can wake you up and open your world.

Resources by Jim Cain

All of the following books and training cards from Jim Cain are available from the American Camp Association (ACA) Bookstore (www.acabookstore.org) and Healthy Learning (www.healthylearning.com).

100 Activities That Build Unity, Community & Connection by Jim Cain ISBN 978-1-60679-374-9
The world's best icebreakers and so much more!

The Big Book of Low-Cost Training Games by Jim Cain and Mary Scannell ISBN 978-0-07-177437-6
Effective activities to reinforce training topics.

Essential Staff Training Activities by Jim Cain, Clare Marie Hannon, and David Knobbe ISBN 978-0-7575-6167-2
Make your next staff training active, engaging, memorable, effective and fun!

Find Something To Do! by Jim Cain ISBN 978-0-9882046-0-7
130+ powerful activities that require no equipment at all.

The Revised and Expanded Book of Raccoon Circles by Jim Cain and Tom Smith ISBN 978-0-7575-3265-8
Hundreds of team activities with a single piece of tubular webbing.

Rope Games by Jim Cain ISBN 978-0-9882046-1-4
Create an infinite variety of group experiences and team challenges with a finite collection of ropes.

A Teachable Moment: A Facilitator's Guide to Activities for Processing, Debriefing, Reviewing and Reflection by Jim Cain, Michelle Cummings and Jennifer Stanchfield ISBN 978-0-7575-1782-2
Some of the best debriefing techniques ever assembled.

Teambuilding Puzzles by Jim Cain, Chris Cavert, Mike Anderson, and Tom Heck ISBN 978-0-7575-7040-7
100 puzzles for teams that build valuable life skills. Useful for escape rooms and other teambuilding challenges.

Teamwork & Teamplay by Jim Cain and Barry Jolliff ISBN 978-0-7872-4532-0
417 award-winning pages, considered by many to be the "essential" teambuilding text.

The Teamwork & Teamplay International Edition by Jim Cain ISBN 978-0-9882046-3-8
51 team activities, 16 languages, one world!

Teamwork & Teamplay Training Cards by Jim Cain ISBN 978-0-9882046-2-1
Facilitate 17+ teambuilding activities with this unique deck of 65 large format cards, instructions included.

In addition to these outstanding books you can also download teambuilding activities from the Teamwork & Teamplay website (www.teamworkandteamplay.com).

Equipment

The equipment for many of the activities in this book is simple enough for you to create yourself, with index cards, dice, tennis balls, photocopies, playing cards, tarps, ropes, and other easy-to-find objects, available at most discount, stationery, or hardware stores. Several of the activities require some unique props, and all of these are available from the Teamwork & Teamplay website (www.teamworkandteamplay.com) and Training Wheels, Inc. (www.training-wheels.com). The list below will help you identify the necessary equipment for each of the following activities:

Activity	Equipment
The Big Question, Thumbprints Match Cards, Are You More Like?	Teamwork & Teamplay Training Cards (1 deck has 52 different cards)
Hall of Fame Statues Bull Ring Community Candelabra	Teamplay Tubes
Wrapped Around My Finger My Lifeline, The Last Dance Where Ya From? Where Ya Been? Twice Around the Block Believe It or Knot, Pass the Knot All My Life's a Circle, The Meter	Raccoon Circles (1 per group of 6 people)
Five Photos The Virtual Slideshow	Debriefing Clicker
Giant Jigsaw Puzzle	Giant Jigsaw Puzzle (1 per group of 6 to 8 people)
Bull Ring Variations	Bull Ring, 3-D Bull Ring, Goin' Fishin' Tool
Wobble	Wobble Kit from T&T (6 people per kit)
A Perfect Match Lycra Blindfolds	Perfect Match Kit (12 participants per kit)
Petecas	Petecas (Funderbirds) (1 per group of 10 people)

For even more interesting team and community building resources (books, papers, props, equipment, debriefing tools, and more), email Jim Cain (jimcain@teamworkandteamplay.com) and ask for a copy of his most recent "experiential garage sale" list.

ABOUT THE AUTHOR

ABOUT JIM CAIN AND TEAMWORK & TEAMPLAY

Dr. Jim Cain is the author of more than a dozen texts filled with powerful team and community building activities from around the world. His train-the-trainer workshops are legendary in the adventure-based learning world and have taken him to all 50 states and 31 countries (so far). He is the innovator of over 40 teambuilding activities used by corporations, colleges, camps, conferences, and communities. But mostly, Jim likes to share his unique collection of team challenges, games, puzzles, and training techniques with audiences of all kinds.

Jim is also the creative mind behind his active learning company Teamwork & Teamplay, which provides staff trainings, teambuilding equipment, debriefing tools, curriculum development, books, conference workshops, keynote presentations, and teambuilding consulting services around the world.

For more information, visit the Teamwork & Teamplay website at www.teamworkandteamplay.com, or contact Jim Cain at (585) 637-0328.

Jim Cain, Ph.D.
Teamwork & Teamplay
468 Salmon Creek Road
Brockport, New York 14420 USA
Phone (585) 637-0328
jimcain@teamworkandteamplay.com
www.teamworkandteamplay.com

CLOSING THOUGHTS

Over the years, I've encountered some amazing people in this world. Intelligent, talented, vibrant, optimistic, compassionate people that are always willing to share what they know. It is inspiring just to be around them, and my life is better for having known them. Bob Ditter, who generously agreed to write the foreword for this book, is one of those people. And if you have met Bob, then you know I'm right. Michael Brandwein is also one of them, and every time our paths cross, I am richer by far. Chris Cavert, who I mention numerous times in this book, is a living example of the abundance philosophy. So is Sam Sikes, who, aside from sharing wonderful teambuilding activities with me, was also the person who taught me how to self-publish my own books. Thanks, Sam. Michelle Cummings, Faith Evans, Clare Marie Hannon, Steve Maquire, Scott Arizala, Barry Jolliff, Kirk Weisler, Bill Henderson, Larry Hall, Gwynn Powell, Linda Pulliam, Mike Lim, Karl Rohnke, Tom and Jen Leahy, the list goes on and on and on. I love you guys.

But today I want to share with you one bit of wisdom that I believe is particularly significant given the content of this book, and I have Tom Andrews to thank for sharing this information with me. Please read carefully. This information applies to you!

#1: I respect you. As the reader of this book, I know what you do. Heck, I do what you do. And I respect you for doing it.

#2: Because I respect you, I am going to share with you the very best knowledge, tools, activities, and information that I know, holding nothing back.

#3: Because I respect you and because I've shared the best information that I know with you, I intend to hold you responsible for using this information to improve the world. It is not enough to simply know these things; our world absolutely needs you to apply what you have learned here. There is no better time or place to implement what you have learned here about building unity, community, and connection. Go now. Start with what you have, start with where you are. If you've been waiting for a sign to begin, this is it.

Go!

Best wishes and good luck,
Jim Cain
Teamwork & Teamplay